The Mac OS X 10.6 Snow Leopard **Pocket**Guide

Jeff**Carlson**

Ginormous knowledge, pocket sized.

Peachpit Press

The Mac OS X 10.6 Snow Leopard Pocket Guide
Jeff Carlson

Peachpit Press
1249 Eighth Street
Berkeley, CA 94710
510/524-2178
510/524-2221 (fax)

Find us on the Web at: www.peachpit.com
To report errors, please send a note to errata@peachpit.com

Peachpit Press is a division of Pearson Education.

Copyright © 2010 by Jeff Carlson

Editor: Clifford Colby
Copyeditor: Liane Thomas
Production editor: Cory Borman
Compositor: Jeff Carlson
Indexer: Ann Rogers
Cover design and photography: Aren Howell
Interior design: Kim Scott, with Maureen Forys

005.446

C19M

2010

ISBN-13:   978-0-321-64689-7
ISBN-10:   0-321-64689-4

9 8 7 6 5 4 3 2 1

Printed and bound in the United States of America

For Ellie, Ainsley, Mazama, Elliott, Olive, Zoe, Amy, and Anna

Acknowledgments

You probably have an image in your head of a book writer: holed up in an attic office space, alone, sleep-deprived, heading downstairs occasionally for coffee and sugar and the stray bit of protein. Well, yeah, that's pretty much true. However, I wasn't alone. Physically alone at times, but always connected to a fantastic group of people who helped make it possible and who have my thanks:

Glenn Fleishman contributed his considerable expertise, writing chapters 8 and 10 when I realized that it wasn't possible to clone myself.

My editorial team provided every resource I needed: Cliff Colby, Becky Morgan, and Cory Borman at Peachpit Press; my copyeditor Liane Thomas; and my indexer Ann Rogers.

Teresa Brewer and Keri Walker at Apple answered my questions and provided me with review equipment for my *Seattle Times* column, which indirectly aided the creation of this book.

My friends Andrew Laurence and Agen G. N. Schmitz let me bounce around ideas at all hours and helped with some technical questions.

Kim Ricketts, Laurence Chen, and Hillary Vonckx gave me a reason to come into our shared office space and not sequester myself in my home office.

Adam and Tonya Engst at *TidBITS* provided schedule flexibility when it was needed so I could jump on this project when it came up.

Kim Carlson and Eliana Carlson brought me joy (and candy!) as I juggled the roles of husband, father, and author on a tight timeline.

About Jeff Carlson

Jeff Carlson gave up an opportunity to intern at a design firm during college because they really just wanted someone tall to play on their volleyball team. In the intervening years, he's been a designer and writer, authoring best-selling books on the Macintosh, Web design, video editing, and digital photography. He's currently a columnist for the *Seattle Times*, the managing editor of the respected electronic newsletter *TidBITS* (www.tidbits.com), and consumes almost too much coffee. Almost.

Find more information about him at jeffcarlson.com and neverenoughcoffee.com, and follow him on Twitter at @jeffcarlson.

Contents

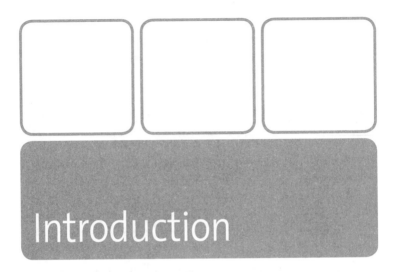

Introduction

Mac OS X 10.6 Snow Leopard is an intriguing beast. It's the most recent version of a major computer operating system, but there are few new "features," in terms of items you can list on the back of a retail package. In contrast, the previous version, Mac OS X 10.5 Leopard, added capabilities such as Time Machine, Quick Look, and Spaces.

But Snow Leopard isn't some humdrum update. The new operating system makes fundamental changes under the hood, with improved 64-bit support, OpenCL, and Grand Central Dispatch (see Chapter 2 to learn what those are and why they're important).

Apple also rolled in a large number of enhancements to existing features. For example, the Finder has (at last) been updated to take full advantage of the Mac's modern processors. iChat video is improved. QuickTime X is more user-friendly and offers the capability to quickly trim video and audio. And that's just scratching the surface. With all the changes and improvements, Snow Leopard feels more responsive and faster than Leopard overall, even if you're not running it on the latest hardware.

How to Get Snow Leopard

If you've just purchased a new Mac, congratulations! Snow Leopard is already installed. If you want to upgrade, pricing for existing Macs is as follows:

- If you're currently running Mac OS X 10.5 Leopard, you can buy Snow Leopard for $29 from Apple or authorized Apple outlets. A Family Pack with licenses good for up to five computers in the same household is available for $49.

- If you bought a Mac after June 8, 2009, you can purchase Snow Leopard for $9.95; see Apple's Mac OS X Up to Date page (www.apple.com/macosx/uptodate/) for more information.

- If you're still running Mac OS X 10.4 Tiger, you need to purchase the Mac Box Set for $169 (or as a family pack for $229), which also includes iLife '09 and iWork '09.

Will Your Mac Run Snow Leopard?

Snow Leopard requires a Mac with an Intel processor—a significant break from earlier versions of Mac OS X, which ran on PowerPC processors. (Apple switched its entire Mac line to Intel chips in 2006, but, until Snow Leopard, continued to build Mac OS X to run on both Intel and PowerPC processors.)

If you own a MacBook, MacBook Pro, or Mac Pro, those are all Intel-based; iBook, PowerBook, and Power Mac lines are not. The iMac and Mac mini made the switch with their names intact; if you're not sure what processor is in your Mac, go to the Apple menu and choose About This Mac (**Figure i.1**).

Figure i.1
Discovering your Mac's processor.

Processor ——

About This Mac

Mac OS X
Version 10.5.7

(Software Update...)

Processor 2.33 GHz Intel Core 2 Duo

Memory 3 GB 667 MHz DDR2 SDRAM

Startup Disk WinterX

(More Info...)

TM & © 1983-2009 Apple Inc.
All Rights Reserved.

How Big Is Your Pocket?

I don't cover absolutely every aspect of Mac OS X 10.6 in this book; there's just too much information for a Pocket Guide (and none of *my* pockets are large enough to carry a 500-page book). Therefore, I've focused on what I believe are the most important—or just plain cool—elements of Snow Leopard. If you're looking for a more thorough reference, I highly recommend Maria Langer's *Mac OS X 10.6 Snow Leopard: Visual QuickStart Guide*.

I'm also making some assumptions: You know how to turn on your computer, operate the mouse or trackpad, and take precautions such as not resting open beverages directly on the keyboard (I mean, balancing a martini on the top edge of your iMac is one thing, but keep it away from the keyboard for heaven's sake!).

As this isn't a basic-level guide, I'll also assume that you know some of the core actions of using a computer in the twenty-first century, such as starting up and shutting down your Mac, accessing menu items (single-click a menu name that appears at the top of the screen to reveal its list of options) and double-clicking an application to launch it.

> **note** Actually, I often see people confused between clicking and double-clicking items, so here's the deal: Click once to *select* something (such as a document file); double-click the item to *open* it.

Conventions Used in This Book

- When I talk about accessing a command from the menus that appear in every program, I separate each component using an angle-bracket (>) character. For example, "choose File > Open" means "click the File menu item, then choose Open from the list that appears." A succession of commands indicate submenus: "choose Go > iDisk > My iDisk" translates to "click the Go menu, then the iDisk item, and then the My iDisk item that appears in the submenu."

- When I refer to a "preference pane," I'm talking about the options found in System Preferences. Choose System Preferences from the Apple ( ) menu, or click its icon in the Dock. To access the "Network preference pane," for example, open System Preferences and click the Network icon.

- Keyboard shortcuts are expressed with the name of a modifier key and another key that must be pressed at the same time, such as, "Press Command-S to save the file." However, the Command key has always been a source of confusion: the key often appears with a ⌘ or ⌃ symbol.

- In a few places I refer to more information found in the Mac Help files. Choose Mac Help from the Help menu.

1

Meet Snow Leopard

Apple is known for its outstanding industrial design, from the first eye-catching and colorful iMacs to the svelte MacBook Air. But here's the hiding-in-plain-sight secret about the Mac: no matter what computer you're on, you interact with its operating system, Mac OS X. A Mac Pro could just as easily be a large gray box under your desk and you'd still get the full Mac experience thanks to the software that runs the machine.

Mac OS X 10.6 Snow Leopard is what I like to think of as a *major incremental* update. It doesn't seem very different than Mac OS X 10.5 Leopard, but it introduces significant under-the-hood changes that contribute to improved performance and a better experience for you. If you're already familiar with Leopard, a few Snow Leopard features, such as QuickTime X, will be noticeably different. If you're new to the Mac, you'll find Mac OS X to be inviting, speedy, and easy to use.

This chapter details some of the major features of Snow Leopard, especially improvements like Grand Central Dispatch that represent technological leaps but which aren't obvious in day-to-day use.

Under-the-Hood Improvements

In the field of video cameras, one of the hottest developments is the RED ONE camera, which records at 4K resolution (more than four times that of typical high-definition). The camera's capabilities are extremely important for people shooting and editing the footage, but when you're in a theater, you probably won't be able to tell what camera shot the movie. You will note that the movie may have good color fidelity or especially clear slow-motion scenes. The technology used to make the film is impressive, but average moviegoers don't need to know the finer details of the camera's color gamut or the rate at which it writes each frame of image data.

Likewise, Snow Leopard's most important advances are in areas that no average person should care about—seriously. What you will notice, however, is better performance compared to previous versions of Mac OS X, especially as developers start taking full advantage of the improvements in three core technologies: 64-bit support, Grand Central Dispatch, and Open CL.

64-bit support

The term "64-bit" refers to the size of each data chunk that can be addressed and processed at one time. Mac OS X 10.5 Leopard and earlier operating sysems were built around 32-bit architectures, and therefore couldn't handle the most modern applications as efficiently.

The practical upshots to 64-bit compatibility are speed and memory handling. Under Snow Leopard, most of the main system applications are 64-bit and capable of taking full advantage of today's (and tomorrow's) processors. That translates to a performance boost throughout the operating system.

The effect on memory is more dramatic. Due to architectural constraints, 32-bit applications can use only 4 gigabytes (GB) of memory at a time. For most programs, that isn't really a limitation, but for others—such as video editing, image editing, and scientific applications—accessing larger chunks of memory can significantly speed up their processing tasks. Snow Leopard can access a theoretical 16 billion gigabytes of memory. Back in the real world, it's technically possible to equip a single Mac with up to 16 terabytes (about 16,000 GB) of RAM, although currently the top-of-the-line Mac Pro maxes out at 32 GB of RAM.

Grand Central Dispatch

The Intel processors in modern Macs get their performance by utilizing multiple cores, or discrete processors that act together. For example, the iMac (as of this writing) is powered by an Intel Core 2 Duo processor, which contains two cores, while the Mac Pro uses one or two quad-core Intel Xeon processors, depending on the configuration.

The problem with multiple cores (and in some machines, more than one multiple-core processor) is that it's difficult to write software that takes full advantage of them. You end up with a lot of processing power that's rarely used.

Grand Central Dispatch is a technology that helps developers reclaim that power by efficiently directing each program's instructions to the multiple cores. At the same time, Grand Central Dispatch does a better job of juggling several applications at once, pulling resources from programs that aren't doing much in the background and making them available to active programs.

The practical advantage is increased performance in applications that use the multiple cores already present in your Mac.

note **Some performance increases may not happen immediately. Companies will incorporate the new technologies into free or paid upgrades to their software.**

Open CL

All this talk of multiple cores steals attention from an area that's seeing a lot of advancement: graphics processors. Most Macs include a separate graphics card that handles most of what's drawn on the screen. (Some models, like the MacBook, feature graphics processors integrated with the central processor.) Powerful graphics cards enable better 3D graphics for games and increased performance in graphics-intensive programs such as Apple's Motion or Adobe's Photoshop. However, current graphics cards offer a huge amount of extra processing power that isn't being utilitized for most everyday tasks.

Open CL (short for the generic Open Computing Language) is a technology that lets developers use graphics processes without having to create their own code from scratch. The language is still new, so there likely won't be too many applications that take advantage of it right away, but the foundations for it are already built into Snow Leopard.

Visible Changes

64-bit support, Grand Central Dispatch, and Open CL are technologies designed for developers, but what does Snow Leopard offer you and me aside from performance gains? Support for Microsoft Exchange Server is a brand new feature, but other changes are improvements on existing Leopard features. Here's a rundown of some of the most interesting ones.

Exchange Server support

Many companies use Microsoft's Exchange Server 2007 as the central hub of important information such as contacts, email, calendars, and meetings. Microsoft Office for Mac provides Exchange support, but not everyone owns Office or uses its Entourage program. Apple licensed the technology from Microsoft and provides the smarts for working with an Exchange Server within Snow Leopard.

This capability enables you to take your Mac to work and set it up quickly to work with your Exchange information—without having to ask the help desk or IT department to do it for you. When you set up a new Exchange account in the Mail application, it configures everything for you, bringing contacts into Address Book and events and meetings into iCal. See Chapter 5, "Manage Important Information."

QuickTime X

QuickTime has long been an important underlying technology for the Mac OS, and in Snow Leopard it becomes both more powerful and more accessible. The QuickTime Player application plays video and audio in an unobtrusive window (no more brushed aluminum interface), and now includes an easy way to trim clips.

A new addition is the capability to record what's happening on your screen, so you can, for example, capture a series of how-to steps and send them to a relative instead of trying to explain the process over the phone. See Chapter 7, "Enjoy Media."

Services

The Services menu is one of those technologies you may have ignored. Located under the application menu (the name of whichever program is active), Services was intended to be a shortcut location for tapping other programs' features. But until now, Services was a mess.

Apple has overhauled Services for Snow Leopard, cutting the clutter by showing only options that make sense in a given context. For example, if you're viewing a Web page in Safari and select a range of text, you can create a new outgoing message in Mail containing that text without going to the trouble of copying it, switching to Mail, creating a new blank message, and pasting it. See Chapter 5, "Manage Important Information."

iChat

Performance has been improved for iChat's video chat mode, making it more likely that you'll have clear picture and audio even when talking to people on slow Internet connections. The image resolution is also better than previous versions, reducing the chance that you'll be playing the annoying game of "who's the giant pixelated speaker?" See Chapter 6, "Stay in Touch."

And on and on...

These are just a few of the more noticeable changes in Snow Leopard. I'll cover others as we get to them throughout the book.

2

Set Up
Snow Leopard

Most of the information in this chapter is focused on upgrading to Snow Leopard from Mac OS X versions 10.5 Leopard and 10.4 Tiger. If instead you've bought a new Mac with Snow Leopard already installed, skip further into the chapter to "Migrate Your Information" to get data from another Mac or Windows PC, and then "Manage Accounts" to learn important tips for working with your virtual identity within Snow Leopard. I also cover setting up a Boot Camp partition for running Microsoft Windows on your Mac (yes, you heard me correctly; it's a brave new world!).

Before You Upgrade

To ensure a smooth upgrade experience, and the safety of your existing data, take the following actions before upgrading to Snow Leopard.

- Update your software. Go to the Apple menu (🍎) and choose Software Update, and install any updates that appear. This step is particularly important if any firmware updates are available.

- Back up your Mac. If something should go wrong during the upgrade process, you want to be able to quickly revert to your current version.

  If you're running Leopard with a Time Machine backup, click the Time Machine icon in the menu bar (🕗) and choose Back Up Now. I also *highly* recommend making a duplicate of your hard disk; that's the quickest way to get back on your feet if something goes wrong. Jump ahead to "Make a Duplicate" in Chapter 8 for details.

- Verify your hard disk to check for directory corruption issues. Launch the Disk Utility application (find it in the Finder by choosing Go > Utilities) and click the Verify Disk button. If errors crop up, you'll need to restart the computer from the Snow Leopard disc and run Disk Utility from there, because Disk Utility can't repair a disk that's currently running the computer; see the sidebar "Repairing the Startup Disk," two pages ahead, for details.

- If you own a MacBook Air, connect its external DVD drive (if available) or make sure you can mount the Snow Leopard install disc from another computer. Open a new Finder window; click Remote Disc in the sidebar; double-click the computer that's sharing the disc; and then double-click the install disc icon.

> **tip** For better performance, connect both the MacBook Air and the computer hosting the remote disc via Ethernet instead of via AirPort wireless networking while you install Snow Leopard.

Upgrade to Snow Leopard

Whether you're currently running Mac OS X 10.5 Leopard or Mac OS X 10.4 Tiger, upgrading to Snow Leopard is a fairly straightforward process. Here are the steps, with important notes as we go along.

1. Insert the Snow Leopard install disc into your Mac's optical drive (or make it available via CD and DVD Sharing).

2. Double-click the Install Mac OS X icon to open the installer (**Figure 2.1**).

Figure 2.1
*Snow Leopard
install disc.*

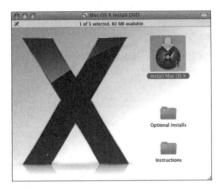

If you're upgrading from Tiger, at this point you need to restart the computer and start up from the installation disc. Leopard owners can begin the upgrade process without restarting (although the Mac will reboot once during the installation).

3. At the installer's startup screen, click Continue, then read and agree to the software license agreement. (If you need to repair the startup disk after running Disk Utility prior to beginning the upgrade process, now is the time to do it. See the sidebar on the next page.)

Repairing the Startup Disk

Disk Utility can't repair a startup disk that's running the computer, just as you can't perform open-heart surgery on yourself (really, do not try that at home). If you need to repair your startup disk, run Disk Utility from the Snow Leopard install disc:

1. Click the Utilities button, click Restart, and enter your administrator password.

2. After the computer restarts, it will be running from the install disc. Choose Utilities > Disk Utility and then click Repair Disk. The repair could take several minutes.

3. Choose Quit from the Disk Utility menu to return to the installer and continue the upgrade process; you don't need to restart the computer.

4. Choose the hard disk onto which you want to install Snow Leopard (**Figure 2.2**). The installer shows only disks with upgradeable operating systems, so you may see just one. If you want to install the software on another attached disk that doesn't appear, click the Show All Disks button and then select the one you want.

Figure 2.2
Choose your startup disk.

Installing onto a Clean Slate

What if you want to start over from scratch? Both Tiger and Leopard installation tools included an Erase and Install option that wiped your hard disk clean before installing a fresh version of Mac OS X. That approach let you start with a clean slate and then selectively add your earlier data (from a backup, of course!). Snow Leopard doesn't offer Erase and Install, but you can still do it: start up from the Snow Leopard install disc and use Disk Utility to wipe your hard disk before installing Mac OS X 10.6. Note that iLife is not included on the Snow Leopard disc, so you'll need to install that separately (from the iLife disc or the Applications Install DVD that came with your computer). Also, if you take this route, make sure you first de-authorize iTunes and deactivate any software, such as the Adobe Creative Suite, that requires online authentication.

tip Earlier versions of Mac OS X installed a huge number of printer support files so you could print to nearly any printer. However, if you're like me, your Mac probably interacts with one or two printers at most. Click the Customize button to access a new option in the Snow Leopard installer that can make a big difference (Figure 2.3). Display the Printer Support options by clicking the triangle to the left and choose one of the following: Printers Used by This Mac (enabled by default) updates only the printer files that exist on your machine; Nearby and Popular Printers installs over 600 MB of printer description files for common printers and for those found on the network; and All Available Printers adds 800 MB of printer files.

Figure 2.3
Install only the printer files you need.

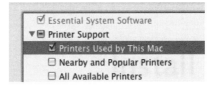

Other Customize Options

The Customize screen in the installer lists the following optional components in addition to the Printer Support files, many of which you can disable if you're concerned about conserving disk space.

- Additional Fonts: Snow Leopard includes fonts for non-Roman languages such as Chinese and Arabic. If you're sure you'll never run across these languages (on the Web, for example), disable this option.

- Language Translations: Install this option if you will be working in multiple languages on your Mac; you can choose which languages to include.

- X11: This software provides a windowed interface to Mac OS X's Unix core, separate from the Finder, and is used by some applications such as the Gimp.app image editor.

- Rosetta: If you still use older software that was never updated to run on Intel processors, Rosetta (which is not installed by default) translates the PowerPC instructions into Intel-compatible code.

5. Click the Install button. After confirming that you want to proceed, enter your administrator password. Now, go get a cup of your favorite beverage and wait while Snow Leopard installs.

   If you initiated the process from within Leopard, the computer will restart itself once to boot from the install disc—don't panic when you hear the restart chime.

   When the installation process is done, the Mac restarts and you're treated to Snow Leopard's Welcome animation.

tip Here's a nice side benefit of upgrading: Snow Leopard is actually smaller than Leopard, so you'll recover some disk space. A default installation (the operating system and included applications) on a MacBook Pro dropped from 18.9 GB under Leopard to 13.7 GB under Snow Leopard.

Migrate Your Information

If you've just purchased a Mac with Snow Leopard installed, the first thing you'll see is the Welcome animation, followed by a series of questions that establish the country in which you live and the keyboard layout you'd like to use. The installer also asks if you'd like to migrate data from another Mac. Choose whether to migrate from another Mac, from another volume (a hard disk) connected to your Mac, or from a Time Machine backup. (You can also choose to skip this step.)

This option is available, too, if you've updated a Mac from Leopard or Tiger and want to move information from another machine. In the Finder, choose Go > Utilities and launch the Migration Assistant. This nifty utility copies your documents, settings, Web bookmarks, and other information that would be annoying and time-consuming to do manually.

It's also possible to migrate data from a PC running Windows, although not by using Apple's tool. See "Migrate from a Windows PC," later in this chapter to learn about your options.

Migrate from another Mac

In the Migration Assistant, or at the screen asking if you want to migrate your information in the Snow Leopard installer, choose From another Mac and click Continue. The installer asks you to connect another Mac using a FireWire cable; Migration Assistant asks whether you'd like to use FireWire or connect over a network (**Figure 2.4**).

Figure 2.4

Migrate data using FireWire or the network.

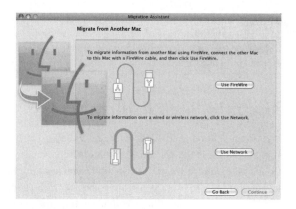

Connect via FireWire

All Snow Leopard-compatible Macs except for the late 2008 aluminum MacBook include FireWire ports.

1. Click Use FireWire and connect a FireWire cable between the machines.

2. Restart the other Mac while pressing the T key, which puts the other machine into FireWire Target Disk Mode; you'll see a gray background with a white FireWire logo.

3. After a connection is established, click Continue. Skip to "Perform the migration," two pages ahead.

Connect via the network (Snow Leopard installer)

The installer defaults to using a FireWire connection, but a network connection is possible, too.

1. Click the Use Ethernet button that appears on the Connect FireWire Cable screen.

2. Connect the computer to the network via an Ethernet cable, or string a cable directly between two Macs.

   You can also connect to a wireless network. Click the Use AirPort button on this page, choose your network name, and enter its password. Then, follow the next set of steps to link the two machines.

Connect via the network (Migration Assistant)

A network connection can be made using a wireless (AirPort) or wired (Ethernet) network.

1. Click the Use Network button. A passcode appears for establishing the connection.

2. On the computer you're migrating from, launch Migration Assistant and choose the To another Mac migration method. Click Continue.

3. On the same computer, enter the passcode (**Figure 2.5**). Click Continue.

Figure 2.5
Enter the passcode from the migration host computer.

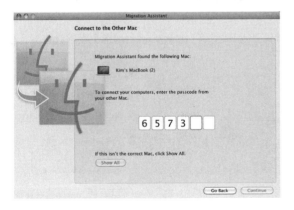

4. Click Continue again to quit all other applications and proceed. See "Perform the migration" on the next page.

Migrate from a Time Machine backup or other disk

It may be easier to restore a Mac's data from a Time Machine backup or from a hard disk that contains another backup (such as a duplicate).

1. In the Migration Assistant, or at the screen asking if you want to migrate your information in the Snow Leopard installer, choose From a Time Machine backup or other disk. Click Continue.

2. Select the disk you want to use; if just one disk is attached when running the Snow Leopard installer, it's automatically selected.

3. Click Continue and proceed to the next section.

Perform the migration

Once a connection has been established, Migration Assistant provides a list of the data on the other Mac, with everything selected (**Figure 2.6**). Click the expansion triangles to reveal more detail; for users, that includes the contents of their Home folders.

Figure 2.6
*Choose data
to migrate.*

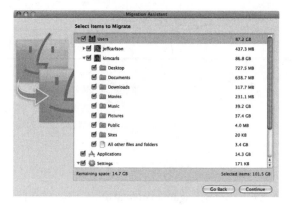

1. In the Select Items to Migrate screen, choose which items to exclude from the transfer. For example, you may wish to migrate just one user account, or not include a user's large Music folder.

tip When you click a user name to deselect it, the checkmark becomes a dash, indicating that some data will still be copied—even though none of the user's Home folder items are selected. What's going on? Selecting any user account copies system and preference files in the user's Library folder.

2. Click Continue to initiate the transfer. Depending on the amount of data chosen, the migration could take several minutes or more than an hour.

tip Be sure to connect the power cord if you're migrating from a laptop, since the migration process can take quite a while.

3. When the process is finished, quit Migration Assistant (or click Transfer if you're still in the Snow Leopard installer).

note When you migrate information to a new machine during the first setup, the account on your old Mac becomes the main account on the new one. However, when you migrate using the Migration Assistant on a Mac that's already set up, your old Mac account is added as a separate account. (See "Manage Accounts," just ahead.)

After completing the migration, you'll need to reactivate any software that uses per-machine licensing, reauthorize iTunes, and otherwise bring your status to the same point of your other Mac before you migrated. As you start working on the new system you may—how best to put this?—run into minor snags where settings may not have transferred correctly, or software that works under Leopard behaves erratically under Snow Leopard. Migration Assistant does a great job, but it doesn't always catch everything.

Migrate from a Windows PC

Perhaps you've just purchased your first Mac, and want to migrate the information from a Windows-based PC. The good news is that it's certainly possible; the bad news is that it's not as effortless as using Migration Assistant—you'll need to move your data manually.

Unfortunately, I don't have room to cover everything involved; entire books are devoted to switching from Windows to Mac OS X. Here's an overview of options.

▪ Connect the Windows PC to the Mac via a network. For more detailed instructions, see Apple's Switch 101 page (www.apple.com/support/switch101/migrate/).

▪ Copy your document files to removable media such as a USB drive, a CD or DVD, or via an Internet sharing service such as MobileMe or Dropbox (www.getdropbox.com). Then copy the files from the media to your Mac. This option may provide the least hassle.

▪ Use software such as Move2Mac (www.detto.com/mac-file-transfer.html), which works similarly to Migration Assistant, copying files, email accounts and messages, Web bookmarks, and other important data.

▪ Connect Belkin's $50 Switch to Mac cable (find it at belkin.com or amazon.com), which streamlines the data transfer via USB and special software.

▪ If you buy the Mac at an Apple retail store, an Apple Genius (one of the support specialists) can transfer your information for you.

Manage User Accounts

When you interact with Mac OS X, the operating system sees you as a *user account*. You may have just one account, or you may share a Mac and set up separate accounts for each member of your family. Although each account shares resources from the system—such as the applications and connection to the Internet—the accounts exist as separate identities, each with its own settings, documents, and other data (**Figure 2.7**).

Figure 2.7
User accounts are separate, but each uses the same system resources.

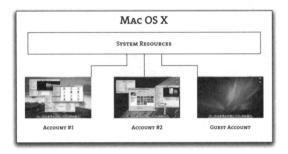

Setting up the first user during installation

The first time you install Mac OS X on a Mac, or the first time you start up a brand new Mac, you're asked to enter information to create a user account. (If you opted to migrate data from another computer, your previous account is used.) Enter a user name, a shortened version of that—the installer makes a suggestion based on the name you enter—and a password.

tip It's possible to set up the first user account without providing a password, but you don't want to do that. Mac OS X requires a password when installing software or performing other actions that are sensitive to the workings of the operating system. For security's sake, assign a password.

Manage user settings

The Accounts preference pane is where you manage accounts and configure whether the computer presents a login screen at startup or automatically opens in one user account. It's also where you can enable fast user switching to run multiple accounts at the same time. To access the Accounts preference pane, do the following.

1. Open System Preferences: choose System Preferences from the Apple (🍎) menu, or click its icon in the Dock.

2. Click the Accounts icon (**Figure 2.8**) to open the pane.

Figure 2.8
The Accounts icon in System Preferences.

Password pane

The Password pane offers options for managing your password and identity (**Figure 2.9**).

- Click the Change Password button to assign a new master password (see Chapter 11).

- Feel free to change your name in the Full Name field. This information is used at login and also when sharing files (see Chapter 8).

- Clicking the picture field brings up a menu with some stock icons, or you can choose Edit Picture to take a photo of yourself (if your Mac has a camera).

tip   You can also use Cut and Paste to change the picture. Copy an image from another source (such as a Web page), click the picture field to select it, and choose Edit > Paste. Use the controls that appear to specify the size of the image and click the Set button to apply it.

- If you have a MobileMe account, click the Set button to switch to the MobileMe preference pane to enter your information.

Figure 2.9
The Accounts Password pane.

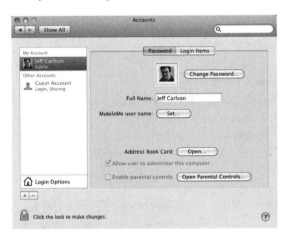

Administrator and regular accounts

You'll notice in Figure 2.9, one item is enabled but grayed out: Allow user to administer this computer. User accounts come in two varieties: administrators and regular users. The first account created under Mac OS X is automatically set up as an administrator, because you frequently need to authorize actions such as making changes to settings (like these account options). Parental controls are also disabled for an admin account, because the admin is the one who has the authority to set the controls.

Regular accounts aren't necessarily restricted—you can still install software and perform other common tasks—but they're not able to change parameters such as system preferences.

Manage login items

Some software packages install programs that need to run invisibly in the background (such as iTunesHelper), while others provide the option to launch at startup. The Login Items pane controls what components automatically run and lets you add others.

Add a login item

Any file—applications, movies, documents, whatever—can be set to launch at login. On my Mac, I've included a Twitter client, a password manager, and a to-do application as login items so I don't have to remember to launch them individually.

1. Click the Add (+) button below the list (**Figure 2.10**).

Figure 2.10
*The Login
Items pane.*

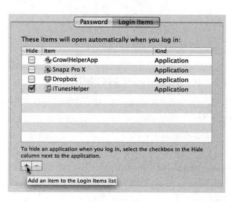

2. Locate the item to add in the dialog that appears, and click Add.

To make an item invisible after it has opened, enable the Hide checkbox.

To remove an item, click the Delete (−) button. As you'll see in Chapter 12, deleting login items is helpful when trying to troubleshoot problems.

tip **Does the Login Items list contain something that looks questionable? Control-click or right-click the item and choose Reveal in Finder to** locate the file, which may provide a hint as to which software owns it.

Create a new account

If multiple people share one Mac, it's a good idea to set up separate user accounts for each person. Their files and settings are stored in their own directories, and they can customize the desktop background, screen saver, and viewing preferences to their hearts' content.

1. In the Accounts preference pane, click the lock icon and enter your administrator password to access the controls you'll need.

2. Click the Add (+) button below the accounts list. A dialog appears (**Figure 2.11**).

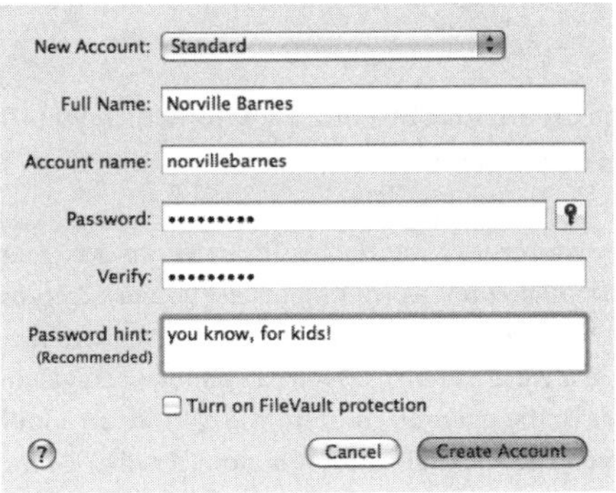

Figure 2.11
Create a new user account.

New Account:	Standard
Full Name:	Norville Barnes
Account name:	norvillebarnes
Password:	•••••••••
Verify:	•••••••••
Password hint: (Recommended)	you know, for kids!

☐ Turn on FileVault protection

(?)   (Cancel) (Create Account)

3. Choose the type of account to set up from the New Account pop-up menu. Standard is the default, but you can also make the account an Administrator or a Managed with Parental Controls account (such as for a child's use).

   The Sharing Only and Group options are used for sharing files with other computers; see Chapter 8.

4. Enter a name for the account in the Full Name field. A corresponding short version is created automatically in the Account name field (all lowercase, with no spaces). Edit the Account name here if you'd like— it's your only chance to change it.

> **tip** You can go back and edit an account's full name, but an account name cannot be changed once the account is set up.

5. Enter a password in the Password and Verify fields. (Mac OS X can help you choose a good password using the key button to the right of the Password field; see Chapter 11 for more information.)

   Also enter a password hint that will be displayed at the login screen if you enter the incorrect password three times.

6. *Do not* enable the Turn on FileVault protection checkbox. I explain why in Chapter 11.

7. Click the Create Account button, after which your new account appears in the accounts list.

> **note** From a security standpoint, it's better to create a new standard (non-admin) account as your main user account, because it reduces the chance that malicious software could take over an administrator account. However, I've always run Mac OS X as an admin user; gaining access to the deeper levels of the operating system still calls for an admin password whether you're logged in as an administrator or not. I'd rather do my best to stay away

from obvious sources of malware (adult Web sites, suspicious downloads, and the like) than to juggle multiple user names and passwords during my everyday work. If you're concerned, by all means create and use a new non-admin account, but I've found it to be not worth the hassle.

> **tip** After you've created a new Standard account, you can turn it into an Administrator account by enabling the Allow user to administer this computer option. Similarly, you can revoke admin status by disabling that option in an Admin account. However, at least one Admin account must be present.

Create a "Bare" Account for Testing

Even if you're the only person using your Mac, you should create a new user account and leave it as unchanged as possible. If you run into a problem where programs are crashing or don't appear to be working correctly, the culprit could be one of your login items or software running invisibly in the background.

One of the first troubleshooting steps to take in such situations is to locate the problem. Restart the Mac and boot into the test user account, and see if the problem persists. If it doesn't, one of the login items in your regular account could be the cause.

Guest account

Perhaps this has happened to you. A houseguest asks to check her email using your computer, but in the process moves your Finder windows, edits your Web bookmarks, or maybe even deletes some files. The Guest account avoids all that hassle, providing a bare-bones, temporary environment. When your houseguest is finished, all changes (including any files saved to the hard disk) are deleted.

The Guest account is not enabled by default. To set it up, do the following.

1. In the Accounts preference pane, click the lock icon and enter your administrator password.

2. Click the Guest Account item.

3. Enable the option labeled Allow guests to log in to this computer (**Figure 2.12**).

Figure 2.12
Enable the Guest Account.

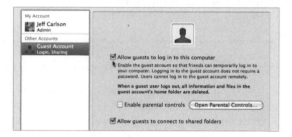

> **tip** You can apply parental controls to a Guest account to limit how some-one uses the computer. For example, you can restrict which applications are launched and set a time limit for use. Click the Enable parental controls checkbox and then click the Open Parental Controls button.

Set login options

Click the Login Options button at the bottom of the accounts list to configure how the computer starts up (**Figure 2.13**).

- Automatic login loads the user you specify; this is the normal behavior on a new Mac OS X installation. Choose Off from the pop-up menu to display the login screen at startup or when you log out of an account.

- The login window can show a list of users or just empty fields for enter-ing a name and password. Choose the latter if you want a little more security (since someone trying to log in to your computer would need to know both the account name and the password to gain access).

■ Showing the Restart, Sleep, and Shut Down buttons provides shortcuts to these commands. When restarting or shutting down, you must still enter the name and password of any account that's currently logged in.

Figure 2.13
The Login Options pane.

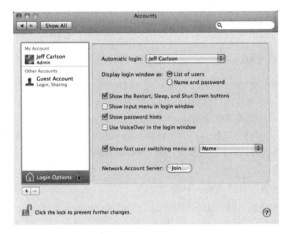

■ Choose the Show input menu in login window option to select from a pop-up list of other installed languages.

■ If Show password hints is enabled, the hint you provided when setting up a password appears after a wrong password is entered three times.

■ The option to Use VoiceOver in the login window speaks the name of highlighted objects.

■ See the next section for more on the fast user switching option.

■ If you're connecting to a network account server, click the Join button. (Network accounts are outside the scope of this book; see the built-in Mac Help about directory services for more details.)

Switch between multiple user accounts

There are two ways to access other accounts on your Mac: log out of one and log in to another, or enable fast user switching.

Log out of a user account

Logging out of an account closes all running applications and processes and "shuts down" the user, but without powering off the computer.

1. Choose Apple ( ) > Log Out *user's name*, or press Command-Shift-Q.

2. At the screen confirming that you want to quit all applications and log out, click the Log Out button. If any applications contain unsaved work, you're given the opportunity to save and close the documents before the programs quit. The login screen appears, giving you the option of logging into another account.

Fast user switching

The problem of logging out of an account is that whatever you were working on is interrupted. A better approach is to enable fast user switching, located in the Login Options pane. This feature lets you run multiple users simultaneously.

When activated, a new menu item appears in the upper-right corner of the screen, which can display an icon (to save space), or the current user's full name or short name.

1. Click the fast user switching menu to reveal a list of accounts on the machine (**Figure 2.14**).

2. Select an account you wish to open. You can also choose to display just the login window (such as when you're going to be away from the computer and want to restrict access to it).

Figure 2.14
The fast user switching menu.

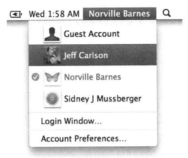

3. Enter the account's password and wait while it starts up.

> **tip** When you log into another account using fast user switching, your current account effectively goes to sleep. It's not entirely dormant, though. iChat, for example, includes a preference to automatically set its status to Away, go offline, or remain open when you're working in another account.

Delete an account

If a user account is no longer useful to you, it can be removed.

1. In the Accounts preference pane, click the lock icon and enter an administrator's name and password.

2. Click the Delete (–) button at the bottom of the accounts list.

3. In the dialog that appears, choose what is to be done with that user's data: save the home folder in a disk image to be read later, leave the files in place, or delete the home folder. Click OK.

> **tip** To delete the current active account, you'll need to log out and log back in as another user.

Run Windows Using Boot Camp

Praising the virtues of Mac OS X compared to Microsoft Windows can be entertaining, but in reality, some people need to use Windows: their business requires Windows-only software, for example. A great but often overlooked feature of Snow Leopard is Boot Camp, a technology that enables you to install and run Windows on your Mac.

Snow Leopard does not include a copy of Windows, of course. Boot Camp is just a framework for installing Microsoft's operating system. But it's not running in emulation: without Apple's distinctive hardware styling, you wouldn't know you were using a Mac.

Boot Camp makes significant changes to your hard disk structure, so make sure you have plenty of free space on the drive and that you've backed up your Mac. Apple's Boot Camp Assistant software provides extensive instructions on setting up Boot Camp, but here's an overview.

1. Launch Boot Camp Assistant, which is found in the Utilities folder within your Applications folder (or choose Go > Utilities in the Finder). Click the Print Installation & Setup Guide button to get the detailed instructions. Click Continue to proceed.

2. Choose a partition size: half of the volume (click the Divide Equally button), 32 GB, or a custom size (drag the divider between the two partitions) (**Figure 2.15**).

3. Click the Partition button to divide the disk. Your Mac OS X data remains intact.

4. Insert the Windows installation disk and click the Start Installation button. The computer restarts from the Windows disc and runs the installer program.

Figure 2.15
*Split your hard
disk into two
partitions.*

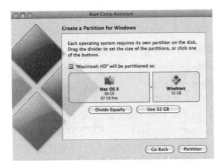

Installing Vista or Windows 7
onto a Boot Camp Partition

When the Boot Camp Assistant creates a new Boot Camp partition,
it's formatted as FAT32, the disk structure for Windows XP. However,
Windows Vista and Windows 7 require the disk to be formatted as
NTFS.

When the Windows installer asks where to install the operating system, select the Boot Camp partition. Next, click the Advanced Options
button. Lastly, click the Format button to convert the partition to NTFS.

Switch between Mac OS X and Windows

Boot Camp does not allow you to run both Mac OS X and Windows at the
same time. Instead, you must choose which environment to start up in.
The Startup Disk preference pane can set your preference, but here's an
easier way:

1. Restart your machine and hold the Option key as it boots up.

2. Select the partition you want to use as the startup disk, then press Return or Enter.

The next time you restart your computer, the Mac honors the setting in the Startup Disk preference pane, regardless of which partition you previously booted into.

tip Although Boot Camp does not allow it, programs such as VMware Fusion (www.vmware.com) and Parallels Desktop (www.parallels.com) do let you run Mac OS X and Windows simultaneously. In fact, they can both use your Boot Camp partition as the Windows environment.

tip Boot Camp under Snow Leopard installs disk drivers that allow you to access your Mac volumes from within Windows Explorer. Previously, a Windows Boot Camp installation wouldn't recognize the Mac-formatted volumes on the same hard disk.

3

Master Your Files

In my years of using and teaching about the Mac, I've run across people who are quite adept in some areas, like using a particular program, but lack some core knowledge about how the computer works. It's as if they missed the first day of a "How to Use Your Mac" class and never caught up with their homework. Ask them to build a spreadsheet in Excel and it's no problem; ask them to locate that Excel file and they're utterly lost. It's not their fault. No one ever said, "Go learn how a hierarchical file-system works." Instead, they learned how to accomplish a specific task—build a spreadsheet, enhance a photo, read email.

This chapter isn't a Remedial Computer Basics class. Instead, I'm laying the foundation of how files work in Mac OS X, and how you can make them work to your advantage.

Your Home Folder

Mac OS X is filled with files and folders, but you can ignore most of them. In fact, Apple recommends you not explore the System folder and other areas that contain crucial system files. Instead, Mac OS X gives every user account a Home folder for storing personal files.

Access the Home folder in the Finder by creating a new window (choose File > New Finder Window, or press Command-N), or by choosing Go > Home (Command-Shift-H). You can also click your account name in the sidebar of any Finder window.

While the Desktop, Documents, Movies, Music, and Pictures folders can hold any type of file, a few of the other folders have specific uses. Library contains settings unique to the user account, so it's best to leave that alone. Public is used for sharing documents with other computers. Sites is designed for building and sharing Web sites. And Downloads is a convenient catch-all location for files downloaded from the Internet.

Aside from those exceptions, the Home folder is yours to use. Feel free to create new folders (choose File > New Folder, or press Command-Shift-N), or stash other files here; it all depends on your level of organizational tolerance. (I like to stick to the basics and avoid clutter—a huge surprise considering the disheveled state of the physical desk in my office.)

tip **Don't rename or move the folders in your Home folder. Many applications (especially Apple's) store files there. For example, iTunes keeps your music library in a subfolder within the Music folder; if you move it, you could lose track of your songs and videos. (However, you *can* choose to relocate the iTunes library; see Chapter 7 for details.)**

Figure 3.1 displays the Home folder in a Finder window. This is also a good opportunity to run through some core components of the interface.

Figure 3.1
Your Home folder in the Finder.

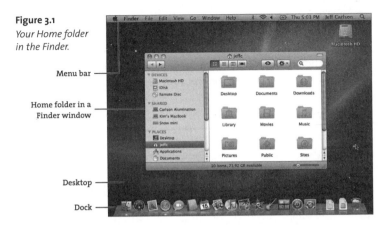

Menu bar ——

Home folder in a —— Finder window

Desktop ——

Dock ——

The menu bar

The menu bar runs along the top of the screen and provides commands, grouped into menus, for applications. You can always tell which program is currently active by looking for the name next to the Apple (🍎) menu.

> **tip** The menu bar is translucent by default, so your desktop background image will show through it. If that's too distracting, go to the Desktop & Screen Saver preference pane, click the Desktop button, and disable the Translucent menu bar option.

The icons on the right half of the menu bar show the status of various programs and processes, such as the strength of the AirPort network and the current time.

> **tip** To quickly remove a menu bar icon, hold the Command and Option keys and drag the icon off the bar. You'll need to go to a program's preferences to add the icon later.

The Finder

When you start up your Mac, the first thing you see is the Finder. It's the file navigation system that lets you manage the contents of your hard disk in floating windows and connect to other computers.

Windows

The significance of windows are nearly lost now, but back when all of our computer interaction involved nothing but lines of scrolling text, it was radical to show the contents of a folder within a floating rectangle. Resize and reposition windows as you see fit, and take advantage of the following window features in Snow Leopard (**Figure 3.2**). (These items can be shown or hidden using the View menu in the Finder.)

Figure 3.2
Icons can be enormous in Snow Leopard.

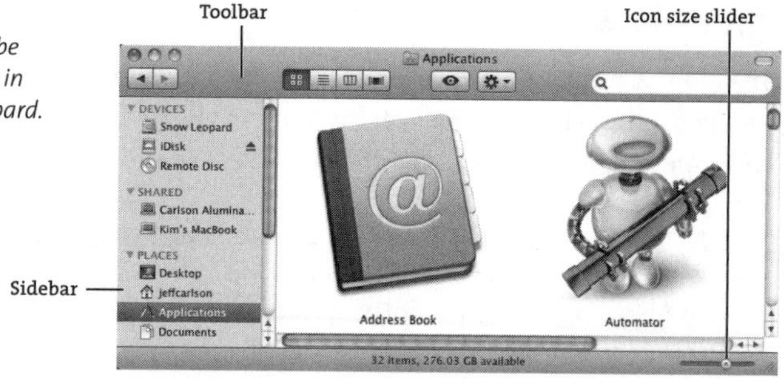

Toolbar

Icon size slider

Sidebar

Window views

Window contents can be viewed as icons, as lists, in columns, and using Apple's Cover Flow mode (**Figure 3.3**). You may prefer one style, or mix and match them depending on what you're viewing.

tip Snow Leopard added an icon size slider to the bottom-right corner of every window in icon view for quick resizing.

Figure 3.3

The three other window views.

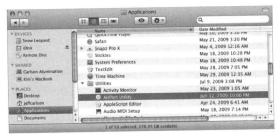

List view

Column view

Cover Flow view

Using icon or Cover Flow view works well when browsing a folder full of images so you can immediately see previews of the pictures, while the list view is good for sorting files by name or by date.

tip When you're in the column view, you can drag the bottom of a column divider to change the width of the column. If you hold Option while you do so, all of the columns resize equally.

To configure how windows appear, including which columns appear, icon sizes, and text size, choose View > Show View Options (Command-J).

tip It's easy to get lost in the Finder and not know where in the folder structure a particular file or folder is located. Choose View > Show Path Bar to display a selected item's hierarchy (Figure 3.4).

Figure 3.4
The Path Bar.

Path Bar

The sidebar

The sidebar along the left side of a window contains shortcuts for many destinations, such as connected hard disks, available network volumes, common folders, and saved searches (see "Find Files with Spotlight," later in this chapter).

Even better, you can add your own files, folders, or applications to the sidebar: just drag one to the sidebar and release the mouse button. (To remove an item, drag it out of the sidebar.) This is a great location to put current project files or folders, because no matter where you are in the Finder, you can access the project's materials from any window.

Helpful Window Shortcuts

Make your Finder explorations easier by using these shortcuts.

- Command-click a folder to open its contents in a new window.

- Option-click a folder to open its contents in a new window and close the previous window.

- Command-click a folder's name in the window's title to view a pop-up menu indicating its place in the disk hierarchy. You can then jump to a higher level by choosing it.

The Toolbar

Occupying the top portion of every window, the Toolbar offers a pair of Back and Next buttons to navigate the folders you've viewed in that window; buttons for the window view styles; a Quick Look button, an Action menu that gives you a list of relevant actions based on what's selected, and a Spotlight search field (more on Quick Look and Spotlight is coming later in this chapter).

The Desktop

If anything is initially confusing about Mac OS X, it's the Desktop. When you're in the Finder, the Desktop is the background space behind your windows, where you can toss files and folders for easy access. But the Desktop is *also* a folder within your Home folder—in terms of structure, that's where the files live. So it's possible to see two copies of the same file in two different visual locations: on the background working area and within a window showing the contents of the Desktop folder.

Think of the Desktop as a room with two doors. I find that I typically ignore the visual space behind my windows (because it's often obscured by windows and applications) and open a new Finder window for the Desktop when I need something there. My wife, on the other hand, almost never opens the Desktop folder, because she knows, spatially, where a particular file appears on her workspace.

tip You'll find plenty of other options for customizing the Finder's behavior by choosing Finder > Preferences. Determine which items appear in the sidebar and on the Desktop, give names to Finder labels, set which folder opens in every new window, and more.

Be a Finder Neat Freak

Some people don't mind visual chaos, while others prefer everything to appear neat and orderly. Here are some tips for the latter.

- At any time in the icon view, choose View > Clean Up to align the icons to a grid.

- Choose View > Show View Options and adjust the Grid spacing slider to move icons closer or further apart.

- In the View Options window, choose an option from the Arrange by pop-up menu to force icons to adhere to the grid.

- The View Options apply to the Desktop, too. Open the Desktop folder in a window, or just click the background, and bring up the View Options window to impose order on your workspace.

Move and Copy Files

Although the Home folder offers locations for common file types, you can store files and folders nearly anywhere. Getting them there is easy.

1. Open two new windows: one containing the item you want to move or copy, and one for the location where you want the file to end up.

2. To *move* a file, click and hold the mouse button, then drag it to a new destination.

   To *copy* a file to the destination, hold the Option key as you drag; a plus (+) icon appears on the cursor to indicate a copy is being made **(Figure 3.5)**.

3. Release the button to complete the move.

 If you drag a file between two volumes (such as between two hard disks, or to a hard disk from a networked computer), the file is automatically copied. You can move the file instead, deleting the original copy, by holding Command as you drag.

Figure 3.5
Copying a file.

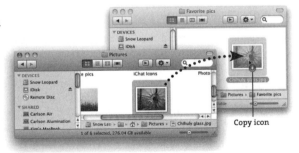

Copy icon

 Another way of copying a file is to select it and choose Edit > Copy. Switch to the destination and then choose Edit > Paste Item.

Delete Files

Discarded files go to the Trash, which, unlike other folders in the Finder, exists on the Dock. Here's how to delete something.

1. Select the offending item in question.

2. Drag it to the Trash icon in the Dock (**Figure 3.6**).

Figure 3.6
Dragging a file to the Trash.

 That said, I almost never drag anything to the Trash. It's much easier to select an item and press Command-Delete to send it to the bin.

Recover trashed items

If you need to pull something out of the Trash, simply click the Trash icon to display its contents in a new window, and then move the file out.

Empty the Trash

Although you may have thrown something in the Trash, the item still takes up space on your hard disk. If you're certain you don't need the bits in the bin, empty the Trash in one of the following ways.

- Choose Finder > Empty Trash. Mac OS X will ask you to verify that you really want to do it; click the Empty Trash button.

- Open the Trash and click the Empty button in the upper-right corner of the window.

- Control-click or right-click the Trash icon and choose Empty Trash from the contextual menu that appears.

- Press Command-Shift-Delete in the Finder.

 If you're using Time Machine to back up your data, you can easily recover items you've accidentally deleted. See Chapter 10.

Securely empty the Trash

Even after you've emptied the Trash, the files you deleted are still read-able to file-recovery software. (On the disk, files are only marked as deleted, freeing up their space to be overwritten later.) To ensure that no one can recover the files, securely empty the Trash by choosing Finder > Secure Empty Trash. Mac OS X replaces the files on disk by writing random data to their locations.

To empty the Trash without being asked to confirm your action, hold Option when you choose Finder > Empty Trash, or press the Command-Option-Shift-Delete keys.

Finder Essentials

The following features share one thing in common: When they were first introduced, I thought they were just eye candy or of limited real use. Boy was I wrong—I now use them all the time.

Quick Look

Select a file in the Finder and press the spacebar. A new window appears with a preview of the file's contents, so you don't need to open the file to tell what it is (**Figure 3.7**). You can view photos, video, audio clips, PDF files, Microsoft Word documents, Keynote presentations, and more. The Quick Look preview floats above your other windows—you can select other items to preview them without closing the Quick Look window.

Figure 3.7

A Quick Look view of a PDF file.

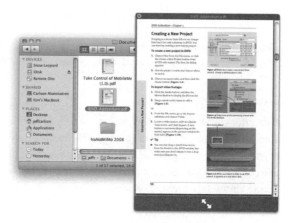

tip Download Quick Look plug-ins that extend the feature to viewing the contents of folders, archives, and file formats not included in Snow Leopard at quicklookplugins.com.

A Quick Look window also offers more options (**Figure 3.8**).

- When multiple files are selected, use the arrows (or arrow keys) to move between them. The Play button displays the files as a slideshow.

- Click the Index Sheet button to view all the files in a grid.

- Click the diagonal arrow icon to present the content full-screen. (Click the X icon or press Esc to exit full-screen mode.)

- For compatible file formats (like JPEG), the Add to iPhoto button appears. Click it to send the image to iPhoto's library.

Figure 3.8
Quick Look
options.

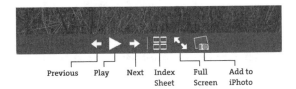

Previous   Play   Next   Index   Full   Add to
                              Sheet   Screen   iPhoto

> tip
>
> **Remember the Quick Look button on the Toolbar? If you hold Option and click it (or press Option-spacebar), you're taken immediately to a full-screen slideshow.**

Spring-loaded folders

When you're copying or moving a file or folder, you must do a little bit of prep work by making sure the source and the target are both in visible windows. Spring-loaded folders enables you to grab an item and move it to a folder that may not be visible.

Drag the item onto the top of a folder, wait a moment, and that folder opens automatically. You can keep exploring in this way until you find the intended destination folder. If you opened the wrong folder, move the item (all the while keeping the mouse button pressed) out of the window that sprung open.

A similar effect works with open windows, too. If just a corner of a window is peeking out among the hundreds of open windows on your screen, that's fine: Drag the file or folder to that window corner to bring it forward, where you can drop the item to move it.

Create an archive

When you need to send several files to someone over the Internet, it's best to wrap them up into a single package that gets transmitted. Select the files and choose File > Compress *(number of items)*. Mac OS X makes copies and stores them in a .zip archive file.

 For more options and better compression, check out StuffIt (www. stuffit.com) the granddaddy of archive tools on the Mac.

Find Files with Spotlight

The Finder turns out to be oddly misnamed, because traditionally it didn't do a very good job of finding files. Starting with Mac OS X 10.4, Spotlight became the central source for searching for all sorts of information on the Mac, not just files.

note **Spotlight isn't just a Finder technology. It's wired deep into Mac OS X and used by other applications such as Mail and the built-in Help system. Whenever you save a change to a document, Spotlight updates its index in the background.**

You don't need to do anything to activate Spotlight; it's just there. Occasionally you may notice the Spotlight icon displaying a pulsating dot, which indicates Spotlight is indexing new material.

Perform a Spotlight search

There are two entry points for Spotlight in the Finder: the Spotlight icon at the far right edge of the menu bar (which is available in all applications) and the search field in a window's Toolbar.

Search from the Spotlight menu

The idea behind Spotlight is that it's quick and unobtrusive. The Spotlight icon in the menu bar is my first stop for searching.

1. Click the Spotlight icon or press Command-spacebar.

2. Start typing what you're looking for. Spotlight begins to display results as you type (**Figure 3.9**).

Figure 3.9
A Spotlight search from the menu bar.

3. If you see what you're looking for, click its name to open it (or use the arrow keys to select it and press Return). The Top Hit is always automatically selected, so often you can just start typing and press Return to jump to the item.

   If you don't spot a match, click or select Show All to view the results in a Finder window (see the next section).

tip   Need to make a quick calculation? Enter it in the Spotlight menu, using an asterisk (*) to multiply and a forward-slash (/) for division. So typing "52*45" reveals the answer (2340) within the search results—you don't need to even launch the Calculator application.

Search within a Finder window

Performing a search within a Finder window gives you more options—
and more results—than the menu bar.

1. In any Finder window, enter your search term in the search field. Or,
   choose File > Find to bring up a new window with the search field
   already active. As with the menu bar, results begin to appear as soon
   as you start typing.

2. Narrow your search, if necessary, by specifying additional search criteria (**Figure 3.10**). This Mac searches the entire computer; "*folder name*"
   limits the search to just the active folder; and Shared scans shared
   disks and connected network volumes.

   Normally a search looks through the contents of all indexable files on
   your computer, but you can click File Name to limit the query to just
   file and folder names.

Figure 3.10
*A Spotlight
search in a
Finder window.*

tip If you find yourself frequently changing the search location, you can
set a different default. Choose Finder > Preferences and click the
Advanced button in the Finder Preferences window. Select an option from the
pop-up menu labeled When performing a search: Search This Mac, Search the
Current Folder, or Use the Previous Search Scope.

3. To further narrow the search, click the plus-sign (+) icon on the search
   bar to apply additional criteria (**Figure 3.11**).

Figure 3.11
Use search criteria to narrow the list.

The criteria pop-up menu includes a tantalizing Other item that's worth exploring. Choosing it brings up a window with all sorts of criteria, such as Fonts used in a document, specific camera settings for images, and much more. Enable the In Menu checkbox for any item you use frequently.

Advanced Spotlight Searches

Spotlight is capable of performing advanced searches, if you know what to enter. Here's a taste of some possibilities; more information can be found in Apple's Mac Help on your computer.

- Include exact phrases in quotation marks ("jeff carlson").

- Use Boolean operators to combine search terms. Spotlight recognizes AND, OR, NOT, and a minus sign (–), which means AND NOT (Jeff NOT Geoff).

- Specify metadata (kind:images author:jeff); Mac Help includes a list of valid keywords.

To really take advantage of Spotlight, download my colleague Matt Neuburg's free NotLight (www.tidbits.com/matt/), an alternative interface that actually taps into Spotlight's underlying technology better than Apple's implementation.

Smart Folders

Here's where you can really get productive. Not only can you perform searches using multiple criteria, that search can be saved as a Smart Folder whose contents are updated depending on the search. For example, here's how to set up a Smart Folder that displays new documents created in the last week (**Figure 3.12**).

Figure 3.12
*Creating a
Smart Folder.*

1. Choose File > New Smart Folder to open a new Finder window with the search criteria enabled.

2. Set the Kind attribute to Document.

3. Click the plus sign (+) to add a new attribute.

4. Set that attribute's first pop-up menu to Created date, and specify that it is within the last 7 days.

5. Click the Save button to save the Smart Folder. Give it a name and, optionally, a location. Make sure Add To Sidebar is enabled if you want it to appear in the sidebar.

No documents are actually stored in a Smart Folder. Instead, it acts as a portal that filters just the files you want to see, updated live.

Hide data from Spotlight

Spotlight builds its index from everything on your hard disk, but you may want to exclude data such as personal correspondence or financial documents from casual searches. Or, you may have a secondary hard disk being used as a scratch disk to shuttle temporary files for an application like Photoshop or Final Cut Pro.

1. Open the Spotlight preferences pane in System Preferences.

2. Click the Privacy button.

3. Drag the folder or hard disk to the list area (**Figure 3.13**). Or, click the Add (+) button below the list and locate the item to exclude.

Figure 3.13
Exclude data from Spotlight's bright glare.

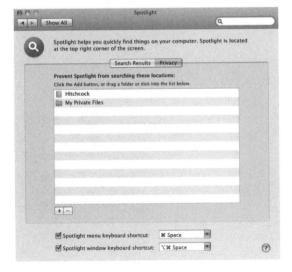

4

Applications and the Dock

Whenever you're *doing* something in Mac OS X, you're doing it in an application. Writing in Microsoft Word or BBEdit; correcting photos in iPhoto or Adobe Photoshop; crunching numbers in Numbers; editing video in iMovie...each application is the difference between interacting with your Mac and having a box of plastic that props up your television.

This chapter covers how to run applications, as well as how to install and update them (a more complicated topic than one might expect). And we can't talk about applications without looking at the Dock, Apple's go-to place for accessing applications (and more).

Launch Applications

Starting an application is known as *launching*, no doubt because in the early days of computers, "launching" sounded more exciting than "wait several minutes while the machine copies data to its memory." Technology has advanced, thank goodness, so now most applications start up in a few seconds. Use any of the following methods to launch applications.

- In the Finder, select an application and double-click its icon. Programs are stored in the Applications folder (choose Go > Applications, or select the Applications item in a window's sidebar).

- If an application resides in the Dock, click its icon there (see "Using the Dock," later in this chapter).

- Click the Spotlight icon in the menu bar (or press Command-space) and start typing an application's name (**Figure 4.1**). Click it to launch.

Figure 4.1
Find and launch applications using Spotlight.

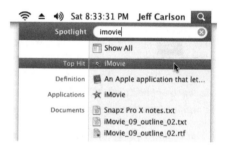

- In the Finder, double-click a file to open it; the application associated with that file launches if it's not already running.

- With an application or file selected, press Command-down arrow or choose File > Open (Command-O).

Open files using a different application

When you double-click a file in the Finder, which application will open it? The answer depends on the filename extension. Some formats are specific to one application; others, such as those ending in .pdf or .doc, can be read by many programs.

- Drag a document onto an application's icon to open it in that program.

- Select the file and choose File > Open With, and then choose an application. (If the program you have in mind isn't listed, click Other and locate it.) The Open With option appears on the contextual menu, too (Control-click or right-click a file to view the menu).

Change a file's default application

If you double-click a file and an unintended application launches, do the following to change which program is assigned to that file type.

1. Select a file in the Finder and choose File > Get Info (Command-I) to bring up the Get Info dialog.

2. Under Open with, choose an application from the pop-up menu to use for opening that file (**Figure 4.2**). If the program you have in mind isn't listed, click Other and locate it.

Figure 4.2
Choose an application to open the file.

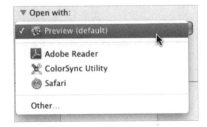

3. To associate all files of that type to one application, click the Change All button in that pane.

4. In the dialog that appears, click Continue to apply the change.

> **tip** I've used LaunchBar (www.obdev.at/products/launchbar) for opening applications (and doing much more) since before Apple introduced Spotlight. I find it to be more responsive and highly recommend it.

The Dock

The Dock, that three-dimensional row of icons that runs along the bottom of the screen, performs several duties. Primarily it's an application launcher, but it also shows you at a glance which programs are currently running. Its contents aren't limited to applications, either: store documents and folders there to access them quickly without digging through the Finder to locate them.

Open applications from the Dock

The names of items in the Dock appear when you move the pointer over them (**Figure 4.3**). To open an application from the Dock, simply click its icon. While the program is running, a white dot appears below it.

Figure 4.3
Click an application's icon on the Dock to open it.

A program doesn't need to be in the Dock before it can be opened. Once any application is launched, its icon appears. When you quit the program, its icon is removed.

Dock Shortcut Commands

The following shortcuts make working with Dock items faster.

- Command-click any Dock icon to reveal the original item in the Finder.

- Option-click an application's Dock icon to hide all of its windows.

- Control-click or right-click an item to reveal a contextual menu containing more options, including a list of a document's open windows.

Choose which applications appear in the Dock

Apple loads its favorite applications into the Dock when Snow Leopard is installed, but you can add, remove, and rearrange icons to suit your preferences.

Add an item

Drag an application (or any other item) from the Finder to the Dock. Other icons politely move out of the way to welcome the newcomer.

note When you add something to the Dock, you're actually adding an *alias* that points to the original. The actual file remains in place within the folder hierarchy.

Another way to add an item is to move it to a new position. Drag the icon of a running application elsewhere in the Dock; Mac OS X assumes that if you're going to enough trouble to specify where you want the program to appear, you want it to stay put.

Remove an item

To remove an application, drag its icon from the Dock; it disappears in a puff of smoke. Alternately, Control-click (or right-click) the icon and choose Options > Remove from Dock (**Figure 4.4**). (The Finder and Trash, and any running applications, cannot be removed.)

Figure 4.4
Control-click an application to reveal options.

Access folder contents using Stacks

The Dock is dominated by applications, but you can put anything into it for easy access. Simply drag a file or folder onto the right edge, just beyond the divider (**Figure 4.5**). One helpful trick is to move the folder containing an active project's files to the Dock.

Figure 4.5
Dragging a folder to the Dock.

 For fast access to your programs, drag the Applications folder to the Dock.

To make it easier to reach the files in a folder, Apple created Stacks. Click a folder in the Dock to view its contents (**Figure 4.6**).

Figure 4.6
*The Stacks
fan view.*

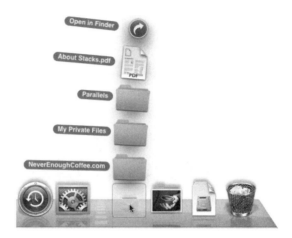

Control how Stacks appear

Control-click or right-click a folder in the Dock to bring up a menu of options, including how the contents are sorted; whether the icon appears in the Dock as a single folder or a layered stack of files; and how to display the content when the folder is clicked:

- **Fan.** After clicking the folder in the Dock, click any file or folder in the fan to open it; files open in their associated applications, while folders open in new Finder windows. You can also click Open in Finder to view the contents of the folder in a window.

- **Grid.** Folders with many items appear in a grid. Unlike the fan display, if you click a folder here, its content appears within the grid. If there are more items than will fit in the window, a scrollbar appears at right. Click the back button to return to the enclosing folder's contents **(Figure 4.7)**.

Figure 4.7
Viewing a subfolder in the grid view.

Back button

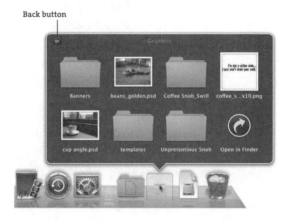

> tip With a folder open in grid view, press an arrow key to highlight the first item. Then, use the arrow keys to select the item you want, and press Return to open it. Or, press Esc to dismiss the window.

- **List.** The contents appear as list items. Highlighting a folder name displays another connected list of items.

- **Automatic.** Mac OS X chooses whether to display the contents as a fan or a grid (but not a list) depending on how many items are in the folder.

> tip Unfortunately, Stacks prevents the one action you would expect from clicking a folder in the Dock: simply opening the folder in a new window (which was the normal behavior before Stacks arrived in Leopard). To do this, Control-click or right-click the folder and choose Open "*folder name*" from the pop-up menu.

Customize the Dock

One of the first things I did with the Dock was move it to the right edge of my screen—I find it gets in the way at the bottom. A number of options are available for customizing the placement and appearance of the Dock. You can find these controls in three locations: choose Apple > Dock; open the Dock preference pane; or Control-click the divider between applications and documents.

- **Turn Hiding On.** With hiding enabled, the Dock slides off the screen when not in use. Move your pointer to the Dock area to make it reappear.

- **Turn Magnification On.** As you move the pointer over Dock items, they grow so you can see them better (**Figure 4.8**). With this feature enabled, control the amount of magnification in the Dock preference pane using the Magnification slider.

Figure 4.8
*Dock
magnification.*

Magnification is helpful when you have many icons, because the Dock automatically shrinks to accommodate them all. However, I find it more annoying than useful.

- **Position on Screen.** Choose Left, Bottom, or Right. Positioning on the edges gives the Dock a different, simplified appearance (since the three-dimensional shelf doesn't make sense along the side).

- **Resize the Dock.** Click and hold the divider in the Dock and drag up or down to make the entire Dock larger or smaller.

Minimize windows to the Dock

The Dock is also a temporary holding pen for active windows. When you click any window's Minimize button (the yellow one at the top left corner), the window is squeezed into a space in the Dock. You can also double-click a window's title bar to minimize it, or choose Window > Minimize (Command-M) in many (but not all) applications.

To retrieve the minimized window, simply click its icon in the Dock.

Minimize into application icon

A new setting in Snow Leopard aims to unclutter the Dock if you tend to store lots of documents there. In the Dock preference pane, enable the option labeled Minimize windows into application icon. A window remains open but doesn't appear on the Dock. To make it visible again, Control-click or right-click the icon and choose the window name from the pop-up list that appears.

tip Hold Shift when you click the Minimize button to watch the window's animation in slow motion. This feature was used in the first demos of Mac OS X to show the power of the operating system's graphics capabilities, and apparently was never removed. Why do it? Because you can.

Switch Between Applications

Mac OS X can juggle more than one running application at a time, but can you? Here are ways to switch between active programs.

- Click an icon in the Dock to bring it forward.

- Click an open document window to bring its application to the front.

■ Press Command-Tab to display running applications as a row of large icons in the middle of the screen. Continue pressing the Tab key until the application you want is highlighted, then release the keys to bring that application to the front.

You can also keep the keys pressed to cycle through the icons. Or, after you press Command-Tab, move the pointer to select the program you want. Or (yes, there's one more), press the left and right arrow keys while the icons are visible.

tip **With the onscreen switcher visible and the Command key still pressed, highlight an icon and press Q to quit or H to hide (or show if already hidden) that application.**

Show and hide applications

As you open more applications, their windows overlap one another, leading to a visual mess. Any application can be hidden from view when you're not using it. From the application menu, choose Hide *application name*, or press Command-H. You can also choose the Hide command located on the contextual menu that appears when you Control-click an icon in the Dock.

The program continues to run in the background—it's just out of the way. You can quickly see if a program is running by looking for the white dot beside its icon in the Dock.

note **When you switch applications using the Dock or Command-Tab, all windows of that application come forward (except those that are minimized, of course).**

Closing Documents vs. Quitting an Application

Here's something I see all the time. A person is finished with a document, let's say it's a Microsoft Word document, and so they click the red Close button in the upper-left corner of the document window. They then switch to another program and assume they quit Word. The problem is, Word is still running in the background; some programs consume a fair amount of system resources even when not active, which reduces performance in other applications.

Apple doesn't make this situation easier, as some of its software (like iMovie) quits when you close its one application window. Getting around this interface confusion is simple: be sure to quit an application when you're done with it. If you need it again, it will launch faster than the first time because Mac OS X keeps some vital information for starting up programs in its cache on disk.

Exposé

Apple has clearly spent a lot of time figuring out how to deal with visual overload as you work. Exposé is another feature I thought would be of limited real use until I found myself often reaching for it.

With a keystroke or a mouse movement, you can separate all that clutter into a sense of order in one of three ways. Then, click the window you're looking for to bring it to the front.

- **All windows.** Press F9 to view all visible windows in an orderly grid (**Figure 4.9**). Minimized windows appear smaller, below a dividing line on the screen; hidden windows remain invisible. Click a window to bring it to the front and exit Exposé.

Figure 4.9
*Exposé, before
(top) and after
(bottom).*

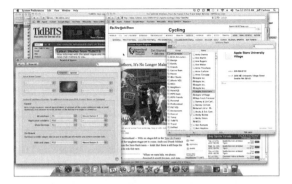

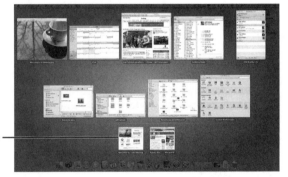

Minimized windows

- **Application windows.** Press F10 to view all windows from just the front-most application. Other programs' windows are temporarily hidden while Exposé is active. When you're in Exposé's All windows mode, press Command-Tab and choose an application to switch to the Application windows mode.

  Snow Leopard adds yet another way to access Exposé. Click and hold an application icon in the Dock for the Application windows view.

- **Show Desktop.** Press F11 to push everything aside temporarily, revealing the Desktop.

Exposé on Recent Mac Laptops

Current MacBook Pro models differ from earlier Apple laptops in how the function keys are laid out. While F9, F10, and F11 still work, you can also press F3 (which is adorned with an Exposé icon). That one key offers all three modes:

- Press the F3 key by itself to reveal all visible windows.

- Press Control-F3 to view all windows from just the frontmost application.

- Press Command-F3 to push all windows offscreen.

- Press Option-F3 to open the Exposé & Spaces preference pane.

tip In the Exposé & Spaces preference pane, assign your own preferred keyboard shortcuts. You can also set active screen corners that initiate an Exposé mode when the pointer is moved to a corner of the screen.

Use Exposé to move content between applications

Hooray, we can view windows using whizzy graphic effects. That's helpful for pulling order out of chaos, but there's more to Exposé than just pushing windows around. It can act as a shortcut when copying and pasting information between applications.

Moving files in the Finder

Instead of spending time getting Finder windows aligned so you can move or copy a file from one to another, shuttle it through Exposé.

1. Select a file you want to transport and move it slightly to tell the Finder it's in motion.

2. Press F9 or F10 to engage Exposé. Alternately, drag the file onto the Finder icon in the Dock and wait a moment for Exposé to activate.

3. Drag the file to your intended destination window and hold it there for a second until the highlight around the window flashes. Exposé kicks you back into the Finder with that window frontmost.

4. Release the mouse button. The file is moved or copied.

Moving other data

The steps above apply to just about any other data you can move between applications. For example, suppose you want to include a portion of an article on the Web (including images or other formatting) in an outgoing email message.

1. Select the content in Safari, then drag it onto the Mail icon in the Dock. Exposé arranges Mail and your outgoing message in a grid.

2. Position the pointer over the message window and hold it there for a few seconds (**Figure 4.10**). The message comes to the front.

Figure 4.10
*Adding rich data
to an outgoing
Mail message
via Exposé.*

3. Release the mouse button to add the content.

Install Applications

When the time comes to install other applications on your Mac, several options await. Even now, decades into personal computing, installing software can be confusing. Here are the common methods of doing it.

From a disc

If you purchase a physical copy of a program, it most likely is stored on an installer disc. Insert the disc into your Mac's optical drive and skip ahead to "Installation methods."

Download from the Internet

Thanks to online distribution, you often don't need to bother with discs (and the bloated packaging around most of them).

1. Download the software from a company's Web site. It will be packaged as an archive (with a .zip or .hqx filename extension), or as a disk image (ending in .dmg).

2. Locate the downloaded file. In Safari, you can click the Show in Finder button (the magnifying glass icon) next to the file's name in the Downloads window (**Figure 4.11**).

Figure 4.11
Locating the installer you just downloaded.

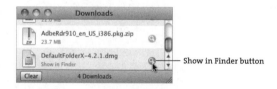

Show in Finder button

You can also open the Downloads folder in your Home folder; Mac OS X puts it in the Dock by default.

3. Double-click the file to open it. If it's a disk image, a virtual volume appears on the Desktop and, usually, a new window appears with the volume's contents (**Figure 4.12**).

Figure 4.12
A mounted disk image.

Mounted disk image

> **tip** Double-clicking the file in the Downloads folder also opens the disk image and saves a step. However, I'm taking the longer route here to explain where the important pieces reside.

Installation methods

With a disc or disk image mounted on the Desktop, you'll encounter one of the following installation methods.

- **Drag and drop.** Simply drag the software's icon to your Applications folder. The developer may have included an alias to the folder in the disk image, in which case you can just drag to that (**Figure 4.13**).

Figure 4.13
Drag and drop installation.

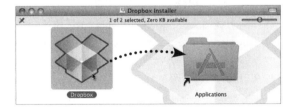

- **Run an installer program.** Double-click the software's installer program, which should be clearly marked. You'll need to provide your administrator password to grant the program access to write its files, and most likely read and agree to a terms of service contract. Follow the installer's instructions.

After the installation

When the program has been copied or the installer is finished, don't forget to eject the physical disc or mounted disk image: Select it on the Desktop and choose File > Eject (Command-E); click the Eject button in the menu bar; or click the Eject button to the right of the item's name in a window's sidebar. You can also delete the original file stored in the Downloads folder.

Update Applications

Software is rarely perfect when it's released. Bug fixes, security updates, and other issues crop up, which is why you'll need to install updates from time to time. Apple uses one mechanism for updating all of its software, Software Update, while other companies typically include update features within their applications.

Software Update

When new versions of Apple software are available for download, Software Update opens automatically and asks if you want to install them. You can also choose Software Update from the Apple menu to perform a manual check.

1. In the dialog that appears, click Show Details to learn what's available. You can also click Install to apply them right away, but I prefer to see what's available first.

2. In the details view, select an update to learn more about it (**Figure 4.14**). If you prefer not to install an update, deselect its checkbox (or click Not Now to ignore all updates). Software Update notifies you if any updates require restarting the computer.

Figure 4.14
Software Update.

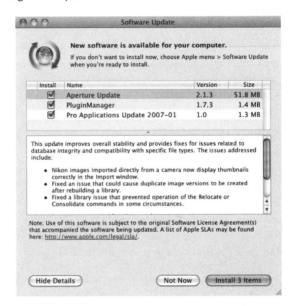

3. Click the Install *x* Items button to apply the updates. You may need to provide your administrator password to continue.

4. When finished, click the Quit button that appears.

> **tip** Another option is to tell Software Update to ignore an update that you may never want to install. Select an update from the list and choose Update > Ignore Update.

tip   Software Update automatically downloads the updates in the background, which can be a problem if you need to control when large downloads occur. Open the Software Update preference pane and disable the Download updates automatically option. You can also disable the automatic update check, or specify how often it occurs.

Updaters within applications

Most applications now have the capacity to check if newer versions are available. Look for a Check for Updates item in the application menu or Help menu. In some cases, you'll be taken to the company's Web site to download the latest version; see "Install Applications," earlier. Other programs can now update themselves while they're still running.

Expand Your Desktop with Spaces

Do you ever wish you could have a wall of displays to hold all the windows and applications you're running? I've long advocated working with more than one monitor (I have an external display connected to my MacBook Pro), but even that seems limited some days.

Spaces gives you a large virtual environment composed of up to 16 screens. What you do with those screens is up to you: run Mail and iChat in one space, then switch to another space containing Pages so you can work without the constant distraction of seeing new messages arrive. Use another space solely for running Microsoft Windows in VMware Fusion or Parallels Desktop in full-screen mode.

Set up Spaces

To get started, open the Exposé & Spaces preference pane and click the Spaces button. Then, click the Enable Spaces button (**Figure 4.15**). If you want to create more spaces, use the Rows and Columns buttons.

Figure 4.15
The Spaces preference pane.

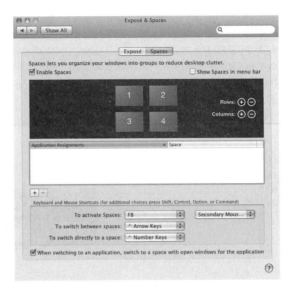

Assign applications to spaces

An application can be assigned to a space, so that whenever you switch to that program, the environment switches to that space.

1. Click the Add (+) button below Application Assignments and choose from the list of running programs, or choose Other to pick something else. You can also drag an application's icon from the Finder to the Application Assignments list.

2. In the Space column, choose one of the numbered spaces.

   You can also choose Every Space, which enables windows from that application to appear no matter which space you're in. For example, setting iChat to exist in Every Space means it remains visible when you switch spaces.

Switch between Spaces

As I noted on the previous page, bringing forward an application that has a space assignment switches you to that space. Here are a few other methods.

▪ Press Control and an arrow key; an icon representing the visual layout of the spaces appears to indicate which space you've just entered (**Figure 4.16**).

Figure 4.16
The Spaces icon, with space 3 selected.

▪ Press F8, which invokes an Exposé-like overview showing all of your spaces. In this view, you can drag windows from space to space.

▪ Press Control and a number corresponding to the space numbers found in the preference pane.

▪ If you've enabled the Spaces menu bar icon, click it and choose a space.

tip Normally, the last option in the preference pane is enabled (When switching to an application, switch to a space with open windows for the application). Turn it off if you want to use windows from one application, such as Safari, in multiple spaces.

5

Manage Important Information

I don't mean to treat computers like people (they hate that, as the saying goes), but there was a time when a computer didn't really care who you were. You'd use a computer for specific tasks: write a letter, balance your checkbook, play games. When you were finished, you'd turn off the computer and do something else.

But now, Snow Leopard cares very much about who you are, because computers are more important for our personal lives. We can use Snow Leopard to keep track of friends and acquaintances, schedule events and meetings, and communicate with people all around the world. Mac OS X includes low-level databases for contacts and events that other programs tie into, which help us manage our lives and synchronize the information between multiple computers and devices, such as the iPhone.

Address Book

The Address Book application keeps track of personal information about your contacts, and also interacts with several other applications: Mail, for example, uses it as the source for storing email addresses; iMovie '09 even taps into Address Book when creating credits in its built-in themes.

Create a new contact

Enter a new record for a person or company.

1. In Address Book, click the Create a new card button (**Figure 5.1**), or choose File > New Card.

Figure 5.1
Creating a new contact.

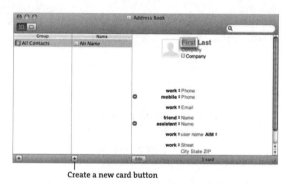

Create a new card button

2. Enter the contact's information in the fields provided. As you do, keep the following techniques in mind:

   ■ Click the field labels to change them (such as "work" or "home").

   ■ Click the green Add (+) button to the left of a field to add a new entry. So, for example, if you want to include a home phone number, click the Add button and specify that item as "home" from the field label pop-up menu (**Figure 5.2**).

Figure 5.2
Creating a
new contact.

Add or remove fields

- Similarly, click the Remove (–) button to delete any unused fields. However, go ahead and keep fields you think you may fill in later. When you're not editing the card, empty fields are invisible.

- The "user name" field below the "Name" fields refers to instant messaging. (Sometimes I wish Apple were a tad more descriptive.) Enter the identity and choose AIM from the second pop-up menu if it's a MobileMe (formerly .Mac) identity to use with iChat. Or, choose from the other options (such as Jabber) if they apply.

- Double-click the image field to the left of the contact's name (or choose Card > Choose Custom Image), and then click Choose to locate an image file on disk, or paste an image you previously copied to the Clipboard. If you're editing the record for your own information and own a Mac with an iSight camera, you can take a photo of yourself. You're then given the option to zoom and position the image as you like.

 When entering phone numbers, don't worry about including dashes or parentheses—Address Book formats the field automatically.

3. Click the Edit button below the card (which is lit up in blue to indicate you're editing the information) to apply the changes.

Import Contacts

Most likely, you already have a bunch of contact information stored digitally—sitting in software like Palm Desktop—that hasn't been updated for years. In your other software, export the contacts to one of these formats: vCard, LDAP Interchange Format (LDIF), tab-delimited, or comma-separated value (CSV) formats. Then, in Address Book, choose File > Import to bring them in. Choose Help > Address Book Help for more information, including ways to ensure that text files import cleanly.

Edit a contact

To edit an existing contact's information, select the card in the Name column and click the Edit button, or choose Edit > Edit Card (Command-L).

Add a new field

Address Book offers many more field types than are initially shown, such as middle name, maiden name, and birthday. Choose Card > Add Field and choose from the options that appear.

That menu also includes an Edit Template option, which takes you to the program's preferences. Choose which fields appear for new contacts, then close the preferences window.

> **tip** A new Address Book feature in Snow Leopard is the Add URL from Safari item under the Card menu. Choose it and the address of Safari's frontmost window is added to the contact's URL field.

> **tip** Address Book is also a label- and envelope-printing secret weapon. Choose File > Print and you'll find all sorts of templates and options for printing your addresses.

Data Detectors

Part of the drudgery of handling all of the addresses and phone numbers and email addresses these days is getting them into an organizational tool like Address Book. Snow Leopard makes it easier using data detection technology, which looks through text to find common patterns—such as the formatting of mailing addresses and phone numbers.

In a program that supports data detectors, such as Mail, position your pointer over an address; you'll see a dotted line appear. Click the attached pop-up menu and choose Create New Contact or Add to Existing Contact to send the address to Address Book (**Figure 5.3**).

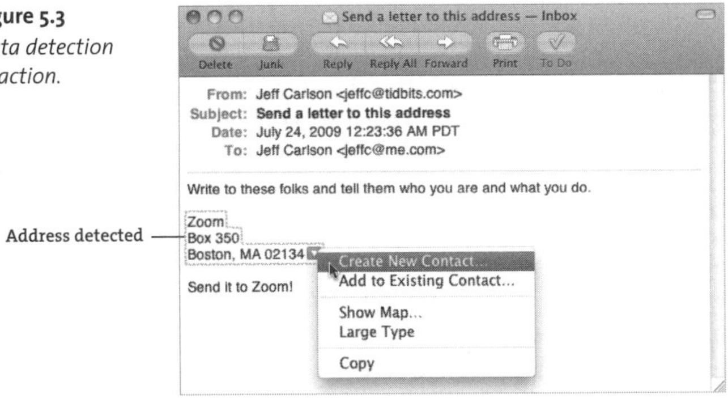

Figure 5.3
*Data detection
in action.*

Address detected ——

Specify your card

When you install Snow Leopard from scratch, the information you provide during the setup process is added to a card in Address Book, which becomes *your* card. To change which card identifies you, select a contact and choose Card > Make This My Card.

Organize contacts into groups

Creating groups in Address Book fulfills that small part of me that likes to impose some order, making it easy to narrow the contact list to just family members or restaurants. But groups are also practical: in Mail, you can type a group name in the To field to send a message to each person in that group. As another example, I also have a holiday list group I use each year so I don't have to come up with the names of people who receive Christmas cards.

1. Click the Create a new group button (+) at the bottom of the Group list, or choose File > New Group (Command-Shift-N).

2. Enter a name for the group and press Return.

3. Drag contacts from the Name column to the group name. Contacts can appear in multiple groups.

 With a group or contact selected, press the Option button. Any groups containing that contact are highlighted in yellow.

Smart Groups

Because Address Book is really a database of raw information, that data can be scanned for your benefit. Smart Groups let the program perform live stored searches. For example, here are the steps to create a Smart Group that lists all family members whose birthdays are coming up in the next 30 days.

1. Choose File > New Smart Group (Command-Option-N), or Option-click the Create a new group button.

2. Enter a name for the group.

3. Start entering search conditions using the pop-up menus that appear; click the Add (+) button to the right to add more criteria (**Figure 5.4**).

   Also set whether all or any of the conditions must be met to include a contact in the group using the pop-up menu just below the group name.

Figure 5.4
Don't forget upcoming birthdays.

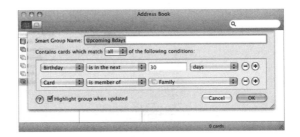

4. Click OK to create the Smart Group, which automatically adds any matching contacts.

   To change the criteria later, select the group and choose Edit > Edit Smart Group; or, Control-click or right-click the group and choose Edit Smart Group from the contextual menu.

Delete contacts

To remove a contact from Address Book, select it and press the Delete key, or choose Edit > Delete Card. If the contact is in a group and that group is selected, a dialog appears asking if you want to just remove the contact from the group, or delete the contact entirely.

If you select a group and press Delete, however, only the group is removed; all of its contacts remain in the database.

iCal

If I don't write down an event, I won't know about it. It's embarrassing
(especially when the event was my mother's birthday), but true. So now
I try to store as much time-based information as I can in iCal (**Figure 5.5**),
which gets synchronized to my iPhone and other machines.

Figure 5.5
*iCal and its
view controls.*

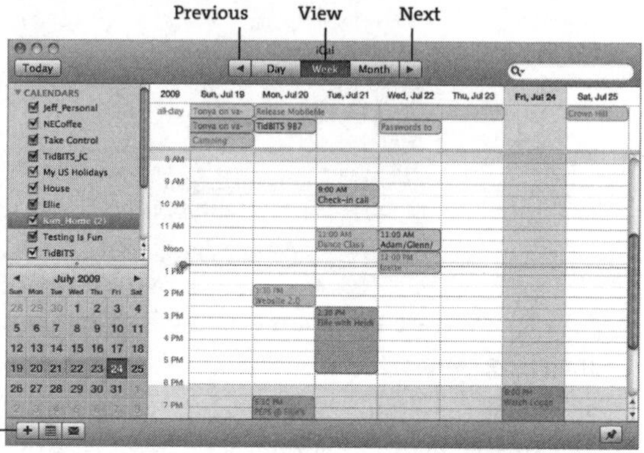

Previous   View   Next

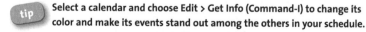

Add New Calendar

Create a new calendar

Unlike the printed calendar you may have in your kitchen, iCal can display
events from multiple calendars. This capability helps you separate types
of events (work versus home, for example, or specific projects).

1. Click the New Calendar button or choose File > New Calendar
   (Command-Option-N).

2. Enter a name for the calendar and press Return.

> **tip**   Select a calendar and choose Edit > Get Info (Command-I) to change its
> color and make its events stand out among the others in your schedule.

Create a new event

There are many ways to create events, such as choosing File > New Event (Command-N), but it's easier to add one in place.

1. Locate the day on which the event will occur. This can be in the Day, Week, or Month views.

2. Double-click to create the event. If you're in Day or Week views, you can optionally click and drag the duration of the event.

3. Enter a name for the event and press Return.

> **tip** New in Snow Leopard, choose Edit > Show Inspector to bring up a separate window that displays the details for any selected event. Otherwise, you need to double-click each event to learn more about it.

Edit an event

Select an event and choose Edit > Edit Event (**Figure 5.6**).

Figure 5.6
Edit an event's time and other details.

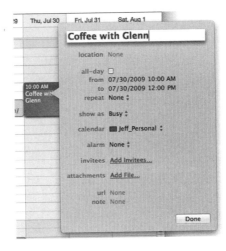

Invite people to events

Whether you're setting up a group meeting or confirming a dinner date, iCal includes the option to invite people to events.

1. In the event editing window, click the Add Invitees link. A field appears where you can type the names of contacts (if they're in your Address Book), or you can enter email addresses.

2. Click Done. iCal sends an email message to your attendees.

Review an invitation

If you're on the receiving end of an invitation, follow these steps.

1. You'll receive an email containing an .ics file attachment; double-click the file to open it in iCal and add it to the calendar.

2. Double-click the event, which appears as a dotted outline.

3. Choose to Accept or Decline the invitation, or click Maybe to acknowledge that you received the invite but haven't made up your mind (**Figure 5.7**).

Figure 5.7
Respond to an event invitation.

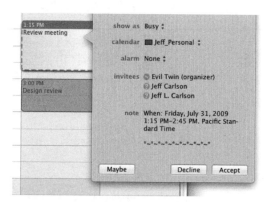

Subscribe to Calendars

You may have noticed a curious omission in iCal: it doesn't include any holidays! A calendar without holidays is...well, it's a freelance writer's life, but enough about me. You can certainly create a new calendar and add national holidays, but there's an easier way. Plenty of free calendars are available online, covering holidays, sports schedules, movie release dates, and more.

Choose Calendar > Find Shared Calendars to be taken to an Apple Web page that offers calendars for download. The files are in iCal's .ics format: double-click one to add it to iCal as a new calendar. If you know the URL of a specific calendar, you can enter it by choosing Calendar > Subscribe.

 Subscribed calendars cannot currently be synchronized to an iPhone or iPod touch.

Synchronize Important Data

These days, it's not enough to have your contacts and events in one place. You want them on your iPhone, on other computers that you use, and available even when neither of those options is at hand. Plenty of possibilities exist for moving that data around; I'm primarily covering MobileMe, but I also touch on syncing with Google and Yahoo, options Apple added to Snow Leopard.

MobileMe

MobileMe (formerly known as .Mac) is Apple's $99-per-year service that allows you to keep important information synchronized among multiple machines and the iPhone.

Set up MobileMe syncing

MobileMe stores a copy of your data in "the cloud," which is a dreamy way of saying "on servers run by Apple." The advantage to this approach is that MobileMe sends any changes you make to data on your computer to the server, which then feeds the information back to all other devices you've set up.

tip Before you enable syncing, make sure your data is backed up. In Address Book, choose File > Export > Address Book Archive. In iCal, choose File > Export > iCal Archive. This step is in addition to any backup system you have in place, just to be sure.

If you've signed up for MobileMe, open the MobileMe preference pane and sign in using your member name and password. Then, do the following to enable syncing.

1. In the MobileMe preference pane, click the Sync button.

2. Enable the Synchronize with MobileMe checkbox.

3. Choose which items you want to synchronize (**Figure 5.8**).

Figure 5.8
*The MobileMe
preference pane.*

4. Choose an option from the pop-up menu to control when data is synchronized. The Automatically item updates the information within a minute or two of when it's changed (no matter which device changes it). You can also choose every hour, day, week, or sync manually instead.

5. Perform these steps on any other computer you own (including Windows-based PCs) to keep them synchronized too.

tip I'll be upfront here: Synchronization turns out to be a difficult feat, and sometimes data gets mangled. (MobileMe started out disastrously on this point, but has recovered.) If that happens, and one of your data sources is still intact, you can reset the data on the server or on your Mac. In the MobileMe preference pane, click the Advanced button in the Sync pane. Next, click Reset Sync Data and choose which data to replace, and on which device (Figure 5.9).

Figure 5.9
*Resetting sync
information.*

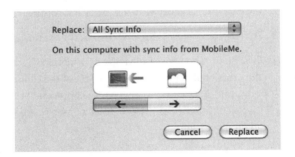

Sync data with Yahoo and Google

You may already use Yahoo or Google to store your contacts and calendars online, in which case you can synchronize Address Book and iCal with them.

Address Book

Set up syncing by following these steps.

1. In Address Book, open the program's preferences and click the Accounts button.

2. Enable the Syncrhonize with (Yahoo or Google) checkbox.

3. After reading and agreeing to the disclaimer, enter your Yahoo or Google login information.

iCal

iCal's sync setup is a little different than Address Book's.

1. In iCal, open the program's preferences and click the Accounts button.

2. Click the Add (+) button at the lower-left corner.

3. From the Account type pop-up menu, choose Google or Yahoo.

4. Enter your Yahoo or Google login information (**Figure 5.10**) and click the Create button. iCal sets up the rest of the connection. The only work you should have to do next is choose when to update the information, using the Refresh calendars pop-up menu that appears in the account's settings.

Figure 5.10
Share iCal calendars with Google.

> **Add an Account**
>
> You'll be guided through the necessary steps to set up an iCal server account.
>
> To get started, fill out the following information:
>
> Account type: Google
> Email address: norville.barnes.hud@gmail.cor
> Password: ••••••••••••

tip   Suppose you want to share a calendar with someone else in your household. I recommend BusySync (www.busymac.com), a utility that makes it easy to share calendars with other people. BusySync also syncs Google calendars, enabling you to see changes in iSync even when you're not connected to your home network.

Microsoft Exchange Server

One of the marquee new features in Snow Leopard is support for Microsoft Exchange Server 2007, a back-end system used by many companies to centralize contacts, events, and email. Before Mac OS X 10.6, you needed Microsoft's Entourage software to talk to Exchange servers.

Now, Apple has licensed the technology to make Snow Leopard communicate with Exchange directly. This feature should make it easier for someone to bring their Mac to the office and just connect without having to schedule an appointment with the company's IT department.

Set up your Exchange account

Snow Leopard's Exchange support can be set up in Address Book, Mail, or iCal. Once configured, the programs treat Exchange data as if it were stored on your computer.

1. Go to the preferences for Mail, Address Book, or iCal and click the Accounts button.

2. Click the Add (+) button at lower left.

3. In iCal or Address Book, choose Exchange 2007 from the Account type pop-up menu. For Mail, skip to the next step.

4. Enter your email address and password. Mail checks with the server and automatically determines the account type (**Figure 5.11**).

Figure 5.11
Enter email address in Mail.

5. In the Account Summary screen, verify that the information is correct and choose whether to link up the other two programs.

6. Click the Create button to complete the setup. When finished, the account is added to each application (**Figure 5.12**). In Address Book, the Global Address List appears as a separate group; its contacts are available for instant addressing in Mail and for inviting to events in iCal.

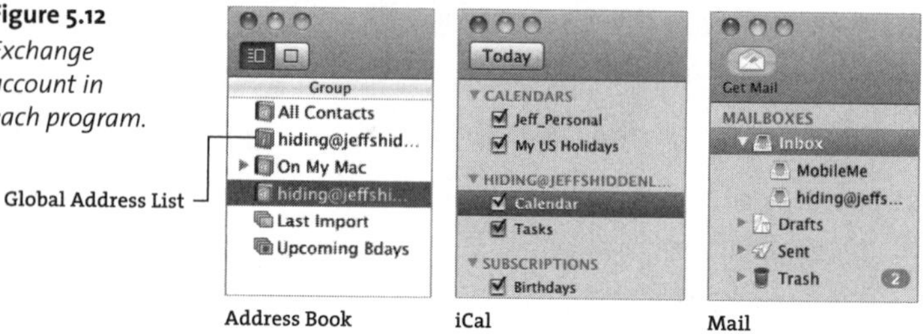

Figure 5.12
Exchange account in each program.

Global Address List

Address Book   iCal   Mail

Work with Text

This chapter has focused mostly on contacts and calendars, but those (of course) are not the only pieces of important information you'll encounter. We probably deal with text more than anything else, in a variety of guises. Mac OS X includes many built-in text features that are used by third-party applications. This section is a look at common elements you're likely to encounter, using Apple's included word processor TextEdit as an example (**Figure 5.13**).

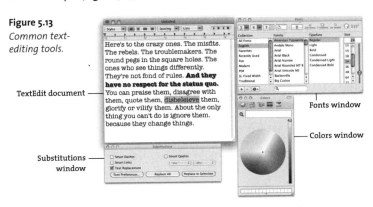

Figure 5.13
Common text-editing tools.

TextEdit document

Substitutions window

Fonts window

Colors window

- **Fonts window.** In TextEdit, choose Format > Font > Show Fonts. The Fonts window sets typefaces, text size, and an array of formatting.

- **Colors window.** Select something, such as a range of text, and click the color picker in this window to set that color. Drag frequently used colors to the row at the bottom.

- **Substitutions window.** Expanded in Snow Leopard, this window contains options for replacing text, such as substituting smart (curly) quotes when you type a straight quote (the default). Click the Text

Preferences button to define more substitutions in the Language & Text preference pane.

- **Dictionary.** Mac OS X includes a complete dictionary you can use for looking up words or for spell-checking documents. The easiest way to look up a word is to start typing it in the Spotlight menu bar field, then select the definition that appears as one of the search results. (You can also launch Dictionary from the Applications folder.)

  To spell-check a document in TextEdit, choose Edit > Spelling and Grammar > Show Spelling and Grammar. You can also choose the next item down, Check Document Now to highlight any misspellings.

 To view the definition for a word in the text, press Command-Control-D over the word in question (Figure 5.14).

Figure 5.14
The in-line dictionary.

Disable the Caps Lock Key

This tip is a matter of personal preference, but I've found it to make me an overall happier Mac user. If you accidentally hit the Caps Lock key often, as I do, you can disable the key in Mac OS X. Here's how.

1. Open the Keyboard preference pane.

2. Click the Modifier Keys button.

3. In the dialog that appears, set the Caps Lock Key pop-up menu to No Action (**Figure 5.15**). Click OK.

Figure 5.15
*Disabling the
Caps Lock key.*

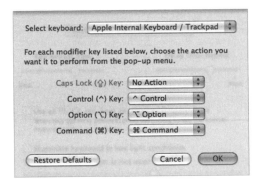

Dashboard

When you need just a snippet of information, it can be tedious to go
to the Web and do a Google search, or root around your hard disk for
the right utility. Dashboard puts handy utilities, called *widgets,* on your
screen when you need them. To activate Dashboard, press the F12 key, or
click the Dashboard icon in the Dock. A set of widgets appears in a virtual
layer above your Desktop (**Figure 5.16**).

Figure 5.16
Dashboard active.

Configure a widget

When you move your pointer over a widget, look for a small "i" button. Click it to access the widget's settings (**Figure 5.17**).

Figure 5.17
Edit a widget's settings.

Configure widget

Add or remove widgets

Dashboard appears with four widgets by default, but more are available.

1. With Dashboard active, click the plus button (+) in the lower-left corner of the screen. That reveals a row of widgets (**Figure 5.18**).

Figure 5.18
Add more widgets.

2. Drag a widget from the row to the Desktop. You can include more than one copy of a widget; for example, add multiple Weather widgets to track different cities.

 Download more widgets from Apple's Web site (www.apple.com/downloads/dashboard/).

To remove a widget, click the close box that appears in the upper-left corner when the additional widgets are visible.

 A faster way to remove a widget is to move your pointer over it and hold the Option key. Click the close box that appears.

Take Action Using the Services Menu

For most of my time using Mac OS X, I've ignored the Services menu. Apple's intentions were good: provide a way to share data between applications without going through a lot of hoops. But the Services menu became a long list of unrelated actions (**Figure 5.19**). Under Snow Leopard, the mess is gone.

Figure 5.19
Services menu under Leopard.

What you see here is only about a third of the menu.

1. Select something—a file in the Finder, a range of text in a document or an email message.

2. Choose Services from the application menu. Mac OS X reveals only the services that would apply in that context (**Figure 5.20**).

Figure 5.20
Choosing a service under Snow Leopard.

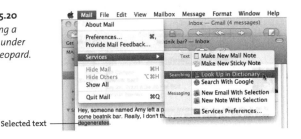

Selected text

3. Choose an action from the Services submenu to perform it (such as viewing a word's definition in the Dictionary application).

Configure services

You can control which services appear. For example, if you never use the Notes feature in Mail, you shouldn't have to view it as an option every time you invoke the Services menu.

1. Choose [Application menu] > Services > Services Preferences. The Keyboard preference pane opens, which includes the Services options.

2. Scroll through the list of services and find the one you wish to disable (or enable; not all services are turned on by default).

3. Click the checkbox to the left of the item to disable or enable it (**Figure 5.21**).

Figure 5.21
Enable or disable services.

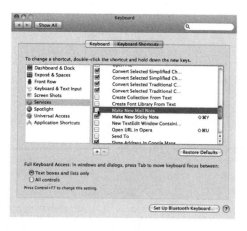

If you find yourself using a service often, you can assign a keyboard shortcut for it that works in any application: double-click the item and then press the keyboard shortcut you want.

4. Close the window to apply the changes.

6

Stay in Touch

Having a computer that doesn't connect to the Internet is unthinkable today. And yet, not terribly long ago Apple was advertising how you could easily connect a phone cable to the iMac to get online. Times and technologies have changed (Macs no longer include modems, for example), but the basics of getting connected remain.

Once online, you're exposed to a firehose of information. Send and receive email using Mail; browse the Web with Safari; connect directly to people via text, audio, or video in iChat. Snow Leopard includes all the building blocks you need to get online and reach out to the world beyond your computer.

Connect to the Internet

Because Internet access is more pervasive today, most Internet service providers (ISPs) make it easy to get connected. Refer to the instructions that your ISP gave you when you signed up for specifics, but generally an Internet connection works like this:

The ISP provides you with a broadband modem that connects to its servers. Your computer is connected to the modem via Ethernet cable or wireless AirPort networking. The modem then automatically assigns your computer an IP (Internet Protocol) address that enables your service provider to send and receive data.

If, however, you need to manually configure your Internet settings, or you know what you're doing, here's how to access them.

1. Open the Network preference pane (**Figure 6.1**).

2. Choose a connection type from the column at left.

Figure 6.1
The Network preference pane.

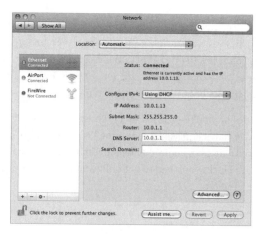

3. If you're connected via Ethernet, choose a configuration type, such as Manually, from the Configure IPv4 pop-up menu.

   If you're connected via AirPort, first click the Advanced button, then click the TCP/IP button to reach the same settings.

4. Enter the settings provided by your ISP. If this is in the AirPort connection, click OK.

5. Click the Apply button to use those settings.

> **note** Networking can be a soup filled with acronyms. Fortunately, Apple keeps much of the terminology away from the casual user. For example, your Internet connection probably uses DHCP (Dynamic Host Configuration Protocol) to assign an IP address. That address likely isn't a unique IP (which are in short supply worldwide) thanks to NAT (Network Address Translation), a technology that gives out local IP numbers as needed.

> **tip** If you frequently take your computer to multiple locations that don't all rely on DHCP, set up location-based profiles that save each spot's networking information. In the Network preference pane, click the Location pop-up menu and choose Edit Locations. Click the Add (+) button to create a new location with the current settings, and then click Done; repeat as needed for the other locations you visit. When you arrive at one of those places, choose Apple menu > Location > *location name*.

Join a wireless network

With a laptop and a few bucks in your pocket, your remote office can be nearly any coffeeshop, thanks to wireless Internet access. Mac OS X is smart about wireless networks, asking if you want to join one when you're in range if you're not already connected. You can also choose a network manually, as follows.

1. Click the AirPort icon in the menu bar.

2. Choose a network to use; the icons to the right of the name indicate whether a network requires a password and show the signal strength (**Figure 6.2**).

3. In the dialog that appears, enter the network password and click OK.

Figure 6.2
Connect to a wireless network.

> **tip** Hold Option and click the AirPort menu bar icon to view a host of technical information about the networks, such as which protocol they use, transmit rates, and types of security.

Mail

I'm a latecomer to Mail, having spent more than a decade relying on Eudora as my email program of choice. When Eudora started to get long in the tooth, I chose to switch to Mail over other programs. (A big incentive was the way I overhauled my email strategy; see the sidebar "My Email Organizing Approach," later in this chapter.) Mail handles email from multiple accounts, and provides several options for managing it all.

Create a new Mail account

One of the great features in Mail is the capability to do much of the setup for you if you're creating an email account Mail is familiar with, such as MobileMe, Gmail (Google), and Yahoo.

1. In Mail, open the program's preferences and click the Accounts button.

2. Enter your name, email address, and password, and click Continue. Mail contacts the server and fills in all of the appropriate information if possible.

    If Mail can't do it automatically, provide it in the next screen and click Continue (**Figure 6.3**). Your email provider has this information.

Figure 6.3
Create a new
Mail account.

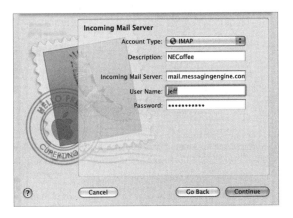

There are two primary account types. A POP (Post Office Protocol) account checks with the mail server and copies new messages, with options to delete the messages on the server or keep them. IMAP (Internet Message Access Protocol) works a bit differently, keeping your local messages synchronized with the email on the server. Although I relied on POP for years, I've now switched to IMAP for easier access on my iPhone.

3. On the next screen, enter the outgoing server information given to you by your provider. This is the data needed to send email. If the server requires a password to send messages, enable the Use Authentication checkbox. Click Continue.

4. If everything checks out, you're given a summary of the data. Click Create to take the account online. Your pending messages are delivered and appear in your Inbox (**Figure 6.4**).

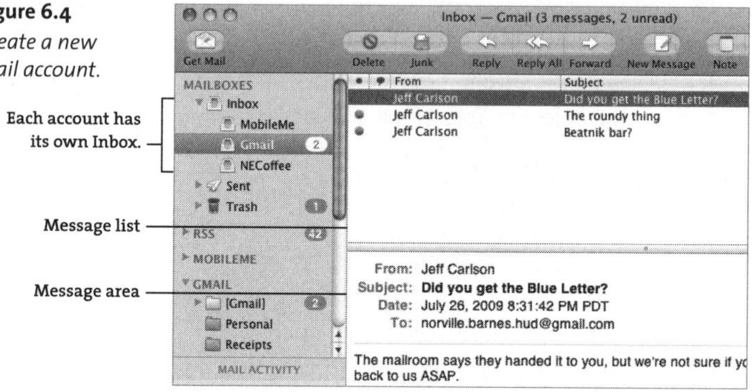

Figure 6.4

Create a new Mail account.

Each account has its own Inbox.

Message list

Message area

> Inbox — Gmail (3 messages, 2 unread)
>
> Get Mail | Delete | Junk | Reply | Reply All | Forward | New Message | Note
>
> MAILBOXES
> ▼ Inbox
>   MobileMe
>   Gmail ②
>   NECoffee
> ▶ Sent
> ▶ Trash ①
> ▶ RSS ⑫
> ▶ MOBILEME
> ▼ GMAIL
>   ▶ [Gmail] ②
>   Personal
>   Receipts
> MAIL ACTIVITY
>
> From | Subject
> Jeff Carlson | Did you get the Blue Letter?
> Jeff Carlson | The roundy thing
> Jeff Carlson | Beatnik bar?
>
> From: Jeff Carlson
> Subject: **Did you get the Blue Letter?**
> Date: July 26, 2009 8:31:42 PM PDT
> To: norville.barnes.hud@gmail.com
>
> The mailroom says they handed it to you, but we're not sure if yo back to us ASAP.

 Once an account is set up, more options are available, such as how long messages are stored on the server and how outgoing mail is handled.

tip For a great look at how to use Mail with Gmail accounts, see my colleague Joe Kissell's TidBITS article "Achieving Email Bliss with IMAP, Gmail, and Apple Mail" (http://db.tidbits.com/article/10253).

Read messages

Click a message in the list to view it in the message area, or double-click to open the message in a new window. If you prefer to just read emails in their own windows, double-click the separator bar between the list and the message area to hide the preview.

Compose and send a message

To create a new message, do the following:

1. Click the New Message button on Mail's toolbar, choose File > New Message, or press Command-N. An empty outgoing message appears with the To field active.

2. Start typing the name of a recipient (**Figure 6.5**). Now you see why we spent time covering Address Book earlier; Mail auto-completes the field using contact information from Address Book's database. If more than one match is found, choose the one you wish to use.

   Continue adding other recipients, and type a subject, too.

Figure 6.5
Create a new Mail account.

3. If you have more than one account set up, choose one from the From pop-up menu. (Optionally, choose an outgoing mail server, too.)

4. Type the body of your email in the message field.

5. Click the Send button to dispatch the message, or click the Save As Draft button to save it for sending at another time.

tip   Mail is set up to check your spelling as you type, highlighting misspell-ings with a dotted red underline. To change this behavior, choose Edit > Spelling and Grammar > Check Spelling and choose While Typing, Before Sending, or Never. Mail under Snow Leopard also introduces a new feature accessible from the same menu: Correct Spelling Automatically, which makes changes as you type.

The Case for Plain Text Email

I'm going to expose myself as an old-fashioned Internet crank here, but let me make a suggestion: Although Mail includes many options for styling text and sending messages with fancy visual stationery templates, *ignore them all*. Most email programs don't render HTML-styled messages well or consistently, so your recipient could end up with a mishmash of images or file attachments. If you care about what you send, just use plain text. In fact, I recommend going to Mail's preferences, clicking the Composing button, and setting the Message Format pop-up menu to Plain Text.

Add an attachment

To attach a file to an outgoing message, choose File > Attach Files (Command-Shift-A), click the Attach button in the toolbar, or drag a file from the Finder to the body of your message.

> **tip** If you're attaching multiple files, consider packaging them into a .zip archive first and sending that file (see "Create an archive" in Chapter 3).

> **tip** Try not to send large files as email attachments, for two reasons. Each message passes through numerous mail servers on its way to the intended recipient, leaving a temporary copy at each one; multiply that by millions of people sending large attachments and we're talking about slow-downs in some pockets of the Internet. Closer to home, it's more likely that a message with a large attachment will be marked as possible spam or a virus and won't be delivered.

Reply to a message

To respond to an incoming message, select it and click the Reply button in the toolbar, or press Command-R. However, the behavior depends on a few factors.

- If you reply with nothing selected, the contents of the incoming message are included and quoted—indented, colored, and displaying a colored line on the left edge (**Figure 6.6**).

Figure 6.6
Replying to a message.

Quoted text ⎯

- When you reply with text selected in the original message, only that text is quoted.

- To send a reply to all recipients included on a message, click the Reply All button or press Command-Shift-R.

tip Never, ever hit Reply All without a good reason and without knowing who else is on the list.

note In addition to replying to a message, you can also forward it to someone else (click the Forward button, or press Command-Shift-F), which quotes the message in the same manner. Another tool I frequently use is Redirect (choose Message > Redirect, or press Command-Shift-E), which sends the message to someone else but keeps the original sender in the From field.

File messages in mailboxes

As your email volume increases, you may want to organize it in some fashion. (Or you may not—I know people who keep all their messages in the Inbox.)

Create a new mailbox

You can set up mailboxes on your Mac or on the server (if you're using an IMAP account).

1. Choose Mailbox > New Mailbox or click the Add (+) button at the bottom of the sidebar and choose New Mailbox from the pop-up menu (**Figure 6.7**).

Figure 6.7
The Add (+) button pop-up menu.

2. In the New Mailbox dialog, specify where the box will reside using the Location pop-up menu.

3. Enter a name for the Mailbox (**Figure 6.8**), then click OK. The mailbox appears in the sidebar.

Figure 6.8
Create a new mailbox.

File a message

Simply drag one or more selected files from the Inbox (or other mailbox) to the desired mailbox in the sidebar.

> **tip** I far prefer using a keyboard shortcut to file messages—after all, I'm using the keyboard for nearly everything else for email—but Mail doesn't offer one. Instead, I use MsgFiler (www.tow.com/msgfiler/). Another utility to check out is Mail Act-On (www.indev.ca/MailActOn.html).

Smart Mailboxes

You'll quickly realize that Smart Mailboxes in Mail are wonderful things. Mail includes two in the sidebar: Today and This Week, which display all messages matching those time frames. Set up Smart Mailboxes using several criteria.

1. Choose Mailbox > New Smart Mailbox, or choose Smart Mailbox from the Add (+) pop-up menu at the bottom of the sidebar.

2. Give the mailbox a name and define criteria (**Figure 6.9**). If a message was selected, the To address is included as a starting point. Click the plus (+) icon to the right of a condition to add another.

Figure 6.9
Create a new Smart Mailbox.

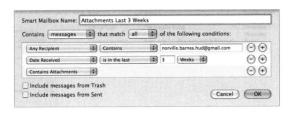

3. Click OK when you're done.

tip **One thing that makes Smart Mailboxes powerful is the capability to reference other Smart Mailboxes. So you could, for example, create one that displays all mail from a select group of people, then create another that looks for messages in the first mailbox dated within the past week.**

My Approach to Organizing Email

Before I switched to Mail, I filed my messages into dozens of mailboxes (most in nested folders) in Eudora to organize them. It was too much. When my Inbox hit around 700 messages, I just stopped filing.

Now, my system is simple: After I deal with a message in the Inbox, it goes to a single Filed folder. I've set up several Smart Mailboxes for current projects and clients, letting the computer go find the messages for me. For example, a Smart Mailbox called "Snow Leopard Pocket Guide" locates all messages in which my editor, copyeditor, indexer, and production editor are included as recipients.

I've also employed rules (found in Mail's preferences by clicking the Rules button) that automatically filter some messages. Email discussion lists to which I subscribe are marked as read and sent to the Filed mailbox, so I don't have to see them in my Inbox; a Smart Mailbox for each lets me view them at my leisure.

I no longer need to worry about where to file messages, and I know that the email I need is accessible via a Smart Mailbox or by performing a Spotlight search.

Deal with junk mail

Unsolicited email is a highly annoying but inescapable facet of online communication. Mail includes a built-in junk mail filter that tries to identify the cruft for you.

Sometimes, Mail needs your help. If you receive a junk message, select it and click the Junk button on the toolbar, choose Message > Mark > As Junk Mail, or press Command-Shift-J.

tip Normally, Mail identifies junk mail and leaves it in your Inbox so you can review it. If you're confident in Mail's ability to filter the good from the bad, you can make the junk disappear. In Mail's preferences, click the Junk Mail button and choose, under When junk mail arrives, the option labeled Move it to the Junk mailbox. You can open that mailbox at any time to search for good messages that were incorrectly flagged.

tip Mail does a decent job of identifying junk, but I prefer a utility called SpamSieve (c-command.com/spamsieve/), which works within Mail and performs better.

Browse the Web with Safari

The Web is nearly pervasive in today's society, as common a communication medium as television, print, and radio. Apple's Safari Web browser is your built-in window to the Web.

note Safari is my browser of choice, but I also run Mozilla's Firefox (www. mozilla.com). Some Web sites use outdated forms or Windows-based software that doesn't play well in Safari but works fine in Firefox. If a Web site isn't working as you expect it to, try loading it in Firefox (or vice-versa).

Access Web sites

Use the following techniques to go to Web sites and navigate Safari's interface (**Figure 6.10**, next page).

- Enter a URL into the Address field and press Return to load a page.
- Click the Reload page button to get the latest version of a page.

Figure 6.10

Safari's major components.

Back/Next   Add bookmark   Address   Reload page   Search field

Bookmarks bar ─┐

Pages in tabs ─┐

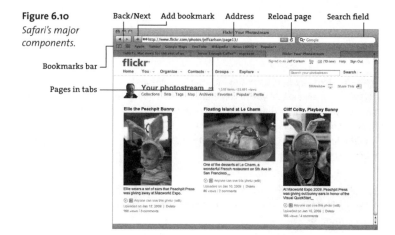

- Click the Back and Next buttons to visit sites you've previously viewed during the current session.

- Enter any text in the Search field to perform a Google search without first visiting www.google.com. The pop-up menu at the left edge of the field displays recent searches.

tip Get ready for the best Web browser tip in the world: Download and install Click to Flash (rentzsch.github.com/clicktoflash/) for Safari, or FlashBlock (flashblock.mozdev.org) for Firefox. Each add-on prevents content created in Adobe's Flash software from loading, which eliminates most of the intrusive, annoying, animated ads on today's Web sites. You can click a blocked Flash object to load it if you want, and add a site to a "whitelist" that allows all Flash from that site to load. Safari under Snow Leopard is more Flash-tolerant— problematic Flash files fizzle out instead of crashing the entire browser. (Apple discovered that the leading cause of Safari crashes was Flash content and worked around that sad fact.)

Tabs and windows

Each Web page can be loaded into its own window, or you can reduce clutter and load multiple pages in tabs that belong to one window. Safari's settings dictate what content loads in a new tab or window—by default it's Apple's Start page, but you can choose other options in Safari's General preferences.

- Choose File > New Window, or press Command-N to open a new window.

- Choose File > New Tab, or press Command-T to open a new tab. You can also Command-click a link on a Web page to open the link in a new tab.

- To turn a tab into a window, drag the tab out of the Tab bar.

 With several windows open, choose Window > Merge All Windows to collect them all as tabs in one window.

 Have you ever accidentally quit Safari and wanted to get back to the sites you were browsing? Choose History > Reopen All Windows from Last Session.

Bookmarks

I've discovered over the years that I don't use bookmarks much; I tend to collect only a few sites that I want to revisit and rely on Google searches or Safari's auto-complete features to pull addresses out of my browsing history. Here's how I add the important ones.

1. Use the Address field to display a Web page.

2. Click the Add Bookmark button to the left of the field.

3. Enter a name for the bookmark and choose where it will be displayed.

4. Click the Add button.

Bookmarks can be edited by clicking the Bookmark icon (the book) on the Bookmarks bar.

tip Here's one bookmark feature I use every day (to check the blogs I manage); it requires a bit of setup, but the payoff is worth it. Choose Bookmarks > Add Bookmark Folder (Command-Shift-N), which creates a new folder in the Bookmarks editing window. Name the folder, then select the Bookmarks Bar item under Collections. Drag the new folder to a new spot in the list of bookmarks in the main area of the window. Finally, add Web sites to that folder. With all that setup out of the way, open a new window and then Command-click the name of the folder in the Bookmarks Bar—all your sites are loaded at once into tabs within the window!

RSS

Want to stay on top of what's going on in the world, but don't want to load a hundred Web sites? RSS (Really Simple Syndication) provides a way to quickly get article headlines and excerpts.

When you visit a site that offers its content as an RSS feed, an RSS icon appears in the Address field. Click the icon to view the contents as a list (**Figure 6.11**).

Figure 6.11
The RSS version of tidbits.com.

The real advantage of RSS is saving the RSS versions of pages as book-marks. Using the technique I outlined in the tip on the previous page, create a folder containing the RSS editions of your favorite blogs or news sites. When you click the folder's name in the Bookmarks bar, choose View All RSS Articles to get a mostly text-only rundown on what content changed since the last time you viewed it.

iChat

Who thought an instant-messaging application could become such a big deal for Apple? iChat began as an interface for sending one-to-one text chats using the AIM (AOL Instant Messaging) network and has evolved into a dynamic, useful communication tool.

Set up an iChat account

iChat can use an AIM, MobileMe, or Mac.com account, as well as Jabber and Google Talk services. (Sorry, MSN Messenger uses an incompatible network and isn't supported.) If you don't already have one of these types of accounts, in Step 3 below, click the Get an iChat Account button to sign up for a free AIM account.

1. In iChat's preferences, click the Accounts button.

2. Click the Add (+) button.

3. Choose the Account Type, enter your screen name and password, and click Done.

tip   A MobileMe account adds a feature to iChat that's otherwise unavail-able: you can encrypt communications between you and other MobileMe members. To activate this setting, open iChat's preferences, click the Accounts button, click the Security button, and then click the Enable button next to the phrase "iChat can enable encryption."

Add buddies

If your account existed elsewhere, you'll see all of your buddies in the Buddy List window (**Figure 6.12**). If not, you can add friends to the list.

Figure 6.12
iChat's Buddy List window.

1. Click the Add (+) button and choose Add Buddy from the pop-up menu that appears.

2. Enter your buddy's account in the Account name field. You can also start typing in the First name and Last name fields to look up the information from your Address Book contacts.

3. Click the Add button. Your buddy, if online, appears in the Buddy List.

Change your status

iChat is an instant service, which means you're likely to get chat invitations at any point. If you'd prefer to advertise that you wish to not be disturbed (but you want to stay connected), click the status menu (which typically reads "Available") and choose Away or any of the other messages in the list (**Figure 6.13**).

Figure 6.13
Choose a status message.

 Setting your status to Away doesn't mean you're unreachable. It's more of a notification to others that you'd prefer not to be disturbed. The Invisible status, however, is another story: you can see your buddies and connect to them, but anyone who counts you as a buddy won't see that you're online.

Text chat

Chatting via text is a good way to exchange snippets of conversation without the potential delay of sending email. If you're on the receiving end of a chat, an invitation window appears, asking you to accept or decline the message. If you're starting a chat, follow these steps.

1. Double-click a buddy's name to open a new text chat window.

2. Type your message in the message area at the bottom of the window. When the other person is typing, a bubble appears (**Figure 6.14**, next page).

3. Continue chatting in this fashion until one of you gets bored or, I suppose, you conclude your conversation. You can then close the window to end the chat.

Figure 6.14
The beginnings of a heady chat session.

You can also initiate text chats with several people: select them all in the Buddy List and click the Start a text chat button (marked with a capital A).

Transfer files

iChat turns out to be a great way of zapping files to someone without dealing with email attachments or file-sharing services. There are two ways to send a file.

- Drag a file to the message area in a text chat and press Return.
- Choose Buddies > Send File (Command-Option-F), locate the file on your hard disk, and click Send.

iChat sets up a temporary direct connection between your machines, enabling a faster transfer.

Audio and video chat

We were all supposed to be communicating on video phones by now, right? Although standalone devices never caught on, iChat serves as an effective replacement. With decent broadband Internet service at each end, you can see and talk to someone on the other side of the world for free.

The person with the best processor and Internet connection should initiate a video chat for best results.

1. Select a buddy in your list; a green icon showing either iChat's audio or video icon indicates your friend's chatting capabilities.

2. Click the Audio or Video chat button at the bottom of the Buddy List, or choose Buddies > Invite to [Video or Audio] Chat. When the other person accepts the chat invitation, an audio window indicates the connection is open, or they appear onscreen in a video chat window (**Figure 6.15**).

Figure 6.15
Video chat.

 If you think an audio or video chat should work but it isn't, go to Video > Connection Doctor and choose Capabilities from the Show pop-up menu. It will report what's working and what isn't.

 Get the family together! Depending on your Mac's processing power and your Internet connection, you can chat simultaneously with up to four people over video or ten people over audio.

iChat Theater

A form of video chatting, iChat theater lets you display other content aside from your handsome mug on your friend's screen, including photos from iPhoto, PDF files, movie files, and more.

1. Choose File > Share a File with iChat Theater or Share iPhoto with iChat Theater.

2. Choose a file or an iPhoto album and click the Share button.

3. When iChat reports that it's ready, choose a buddy and initiate a video chat to start the theater session (**Figure 6.16**).

Figure 6.16
Sharing photos using iChat Theather.

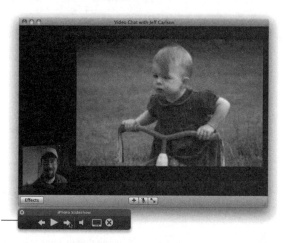

Slideshow controls

> **note** Although functionally iChat hasn't changed much for Snow Leopard, it's another example of how Apple has improved performance under the hood. According to the company, the video resolution is improved and video chats require only a third (300 Kbps) of the amount of bandwidth previously needed under Leopard.

Control someone else's screen

This feature is what helped me convince a couple of family members to finally upgrade to Leopard (and they did so by buying new iMacs, even). iChat's screen sharing feature lets you view *and control* another person's screen (with their approval). It's fabulous for troubleshooting problems that are difficult to describe in email or over the phone.

1. Select a person in your Buddy List.

2. Click the Screen Sharing button at the bottom of the Buddy List window and, from the pop-up menu that appears, choose Ask to Share *[buddy's]* Screen.

3. Your buddy's desktop appears (**Figure 6.17**), and a thumbnail image of your screen is pushed to a corner; click it at any time to switch back to controlling your screen.

   A screen sharing session also acts as an audio chat, letting you speak to each other while you're working on their computer.

Figure 6.17
iChat screen sharing.

Your friend's computer

Your computer

7

Enjoy Media

Within an amazingly short amount of time, the bulk of our personal media has gone digital. Although there are still plenty of people who shoot film and buy albums on vinyl, I would guess that most people now capture images with digital cameras and buy music online or on CDs (which are then often converted to MP3 files for listening on the computer or on an iPod).

Apple has long been a champion of digital media—the iTunes Store is arguably saving the music business—so it's no surprise that Mac OS X handles these media requirements. A large reason for that is QuickTime X, the new version of the core technology that handles video and audio in Snow Leopard. This chapter covers importing the digital media to your Mac and primarily using QuickTime Player to view and share it.

Import Media

Before you can play or edit your digital media, you need to get it into your Mac. Apple's iTunes and iLife applications are the most common routes for doing this, although a few exceptions are worth mentioning.

Music

iTunes has evolved from a little utility that played MP3 audio files to one of Apple's most important applications.

Import into iTunes

If you already have audio files that you want to add to iTunes, do one of the following:

- Drag the files onto the Music entry under Library, in the iTunes sidebar.
- Choose File > Add to Library (Command-O), locate the files on disk, and click Choose.

You probably already own plenty of music CDs—wouldn't you rather store all that plastic in a box somewhere and listen to their music on your Mac or iPod? These steps let you "rip" the music to your hard disk.

1. Insert a CD into your Mac's optical drive. iTunes reads the disc and attempts to get track information from an online service; within a minute or so, you should see the CD in the sidebar and a list of the disc's tracks (**Figure 7.1**).

2. Click the Import CD button in the lower-right corner of the window. iTunes encodes the song data and copies it to the hard disk.

3. Click the Eject button to the right of the disc in the sidebar to eject the disc.

tip   iTunes encodes music into AAC (Advanced Audio Coding) format. To use a different format, open the iTunes preferences, click the General button, and click the Import Settings button. Then, choose another encoder from the Import Using pop-up menu.

Figure 7.1
Importing a CD in iTunes.

CD in optical drive —

Buy from the iTunes Store

I'll be honest: I hadn't purchased a CD for a couple of years before Apple introduced the iTunes Store—I'd been burned by too many albums with one or two good songs and lots of mediocre material. Being able to sample songs in 30-second bursts, and more importantly, to buy music and immediately download it to my hard disk, rekindled my interest.

1. Click the iTunes Store item in the sidebar to view the online storefront.

2. Locate a song you want to buy, either through browsing or by using the Search field at the upper right corner of the iTunes window.

3. Click the Buy Album or Buy Song button, enter your personal information, and wait for the files to download.

tip I won't go into detail about playing music in iTunes, but I do want to share one cool thing. Download Apple's Remote application for iPhone or iPod touch if you have one of those devices (it's available at the App Store). Remote gives you control over iTunes on a computer on your network. I'll use my home setup as an example: My music collection is stored on a separate computer in another part of the house, which sends the audio to an AirPort Express unit attached to the stereo in the living room. Instead of going into the other room to select music or control playback, I use Remote on my iPhone to specify which music to play, no matter what room I'm in.

Choose a Different iTunes Library Location

iTunes puts your media library in your Home folder (specifically, in Music/iTunes/iTunes Music), but that's not always the ideal location. What if your music library is especially large, or you want to make offline backups of your Home folder (see Chapter 10)? To specify an alternate location, do the following.

1. Move your current iTunes Music folder to the new location, such as an external hard disk.

2. Open the iTunes preferences and click the Advanced button.

3. Under iTunes Music folder location, click the Change button and specify the new directory. Click OK to exit the preferences.

tip It's also possible to work with multiple iTunes libraries. When you launch iTunes, hold the Option key until you see the Choose iTunes Library dialog. Click Choose Library to specify the one you want to use (it's the iTunes Library file one level above the folder where your music files are located) and then click the Choose button. iTunes will automatically open the last-used library, so repeat this technique to switch to your original library.

Digital photos

Apple's tool of choice for organizing and editing digital photos is its own iPhoto. However, iPhoto isn't the only option: programs such as Adobe Lightroom or Apple's Aperture include their own importing tools, but in general the process is similar.

> **note** Snow Leopard does not come with iLife '09, Apple's suite of "digital hub" applications that includes iPhoto, iMovie, iDVD, GarageBand, and iWeb. However, iLife is free on every new Mac, or $79 purchased separately, so its programs are often the front line of getting media onto your Mac. If your Mac can run Snow Leopard, it should include some version of iLife.

Import into iPhoto

Normally, when you connect a camera via USB (or you insert a memory card into a card reader), iPhoto launches and displays its import interface. (**Figure 7.2**)

Figure 7.2
iPhoto import.

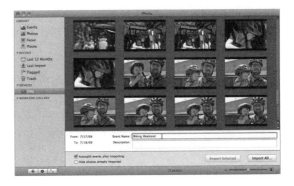

1. Enter something in the Event Name field to categorize this batch of pictures. iPhoto groups photos into Events to help you keep track of

them. If you leave this field blank, the program uses the photos' dates as Event names. You can optionally type notes in the Description field.

2. If you wish to import the entire contents of the memory card, click the Import All button. Or, if you want to grab just a few images, select their thumbnails and click the Import Selected button. The photos are copied to your iPhoto library.

3. When iPhoto asks if you want to delete the photos on your camera, click Keep Photos instead. It's better to let the camera format the memory card to its own settings.

Import into Image Capture

Apple provides another tool for importing photos: Image Capture, located in the Applications folder. If you have a different workflow for importing photos directly to the hard disk, instead of letting iPhoto organize them for you, Image Capture provides a streamlined entry point.

1. Launch Image Capture and connect your camera or media card.

2. Select the device in the list at left; images appear at right.

3. Choose a destination from the pop-up menu below the photos.

tip **Two items in that pop-up menu are pretty cool: Build Web Page downloads the images from the camera and creates a basic Web page, which is saved to the Pictures folder. Make PDF, as you would expect, builds a contact sheet. In the Make PDF application that opens, you can also change the layout of the images by choosing options from the Layout menu.**

4. Select the photos you want and click Import, or click the Import All button to copy all files.

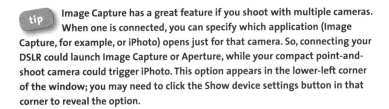

tip Image Capture has a great feature if you shoot with multiple cameras. When one is connected, you can specify which application (Image Capture, for example, or iPhoto) opens just for that camera. So, connecting your DSLR could launch Image Capture or Aperture, while your compact point-and-shoot camera could trigger iPhoto. This option appears in the lower-left corner of the window; you may need to click the Show device settings button in that corner to reveal the option.

Digital video

iPhoto stores casual video shot by most digital cameras, including the iPhone, because usually those videos are short snippets of footage instead of longer-form video shot by a camcorder (**Figure 7.3**). The clips are imported when you import your digital photos.

Figure 7.3
Photos and movies in iPhoto.

Photo

Movie

iMovie

To edit longer sequences of video, turn to iMovie. Like iPhoto, it stores all your videos in one central library; in fact, iMovie also scans your iPhoto library and makes the video clips there available for editing. If you're importing footage from a camcorder, do the following:

1. With iMovie open, connect your camcorder; the Import window should automatically appear, but if it doesn't, choose File > Import from Camera (Command-I).

2. The next step depends on the type of camera you're connecting:

   ▪ For a tape-based camcorder, click the Import button to start copying the data on tape to the hard disk. To find individual clips, use the playback controls to start importing at the start of each clip.

   ▪ For tapeless camcorders, click the Import All button to copy each clip's file from the device's memory or hard disk storage. Or, change the import setting to Manual, click which clips to import, and then click the Import Checked button (**Figure 7.4**).

Figure 7.4
Importing selected clips in iMovie.

Import setting

If the footage is in an HD format, choose Large (960 x 540) or Full (original size) quality, and click OK.

3. In the next dialog, enter a name for the Event in which it will appear, and optionally choose to analyze the video for stabilization (which can significantly extend the time it takes to import). Click Import.

   After the clips import, they appear in the Event Library for editing.

4. Click Done to close the Import window.

tip Obviously, I don't have room to cover iMovie in depth here, but I have a better suggestion: Buy my book! *iMovie '09 & iDVD for Mac OS X: Visual QuickStart Guide* covers everything you want to know about making great movies in iMovie. See my iMovie blog (jeffcarlson.com/imovievqs/) for more information, including a free download of the book's entire iDVD section.

QuickTime Player

In Snow Leopard, QuickTime Player has gotten an overhaul. Where earlier versions featured extensive pro editing features (requiring a separate fee to unlock them), the newest edition is geared for everyday users who want to view, create, and share snippets of media.

Play media files

QuickTime Player has always been a general-purpose "open everything" video and audio player. For example, when you choose to watch a movie trailer in HD at Apple's site (www.apple.com/trailers/), the job is handed off to QuickTime Player instead of playing the video in the Web browser.

tip Apple hosts a page of HD sample videos you can download and play in QuickTime. See www.apple.com/quicktime/guide/hd/.

Download a video file and do the following to play it:

1. Launch QuickTime Player.

2. Choose File > Open and select your video file, or drag the file onto the QuickTime Player icon in the Dock. The file opens in QuickTime Player.

tip Since several applications can read video formats, double-clicking a file doesn't guarantee it will open in QuickTime Player. To be sure, Control-click (or right-click) the file and choose Open With > QuickTime Player.

3. Click the Play button in the playback controls, or press the spacebar to begin playing (**Figure 7.5**). After a few seconds, the playback controls and the title bar disappear, leaving just the movie.

Figure 7.5
A movie in QuickTime Player, with the controller.

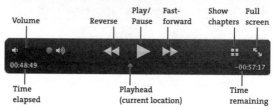

Volume   Reverse   Play/   Fast-   Show   Full
                           Pause   forward chapters screen

Time   Playhead   Time
elapsed   (current location) remaining

Some playback controls appear only in some circumstances. For example, the Share button is disabled when you're viewing a movie with copy protection (as in the example above). Also, when viewing a movie full screen, a Zoom icon appears that toggles between watching widescreen movies in a letterboxed format and filling the screen with the image (which cuts off the left and right edges of the picture).

Stream content over the Internet

Some Web sites offer content as an on-demand stream instead of as a standalone downloaded file. Usually the site will include a link that opens QuickTime Player, but sometimes you may need (or prefer) to enter the address directly. Choose File > Open URL (Command-U) and enter the address. When playback begins, the Reverse and Fast-forward buttons are gone, leaving just Play/Pause. However, you can move the playhead to a location in the movie; QuickTime buffers the content beginning at that point instead of loading everything up to it.

Create recordings

Although iMovie and GarageBand offer features for making on-the-spot audio and video recordings, if you're putting together something quick and easy, you may want a simple utility like QuickTime Player to do the recording.

Record a video or audio clip

Need to send a birthday greeting to your nephew who lives on the other side of the world? Create a recording using the following steps.

1. In QuickTime Player, choose File > New Movie Recording (Command-Option-N) or File > New Audio Recording (Command-Control-Option-N). A new window appears; if you're recording video and your Mac has an iSight camera built-in or attached, say hi to yourself.

2. In the controller area, click the pop-up menu to set the quality of the video, the input sources, and the location for the recorded movie file (**Figure 7.6**).

Figure 7.6
Movie recording settings.

3. Click the red Record button to begin recording. The video controls area displays the elapsed time and amount of disk space consumed, as well as the incoming audio levels.

   After a few seconds, the controls area disappears, replaced by a subtle indicator of the audio levels. Moving your pointer over the window makes it reappear.

4. Click the red Stop button to halt recording. The file you created is automatically saved in the directory you chose in step 2, and opens in the player.

Record your screen

A new feature in Snow Leopard is the capability to record a movie of your computer's screen.

1. Choose File > New Screen Recording (Command-Control-N). A Screen Recording controller appears.

2. Use the pop-up menu to specify settings for the recording.

   If you don't want to record the audio, which includes you speaking, make sure the Microphone option is set to None.

3. Click the Record button. Since the controller disappears during a screen recording (you don't want it in the way), a dialog appears instructing you how to stop the recording. Click the Start Recording button to begin.

4. When you're finished, click the Stop Recording item in the menu bar, or press Command-Control-Esc. The movie file opens.

tip   If you anticipate needing to record your screen more often, such as for interactive tutorials, check out Telestream's ScreenFlow (www. telestream.net/screen-flow/).

Trim videos

Another new feature to QuickTime Player under Snow Leopard is the capability to trim video clips. It's a fast, easy way to cut out extraneous bits of a video clip, such as the first few seconds while you were waiting for something to happen. Trimming affects just one clip—if you need to edit together several clips, turn to iMovie.

1. Open a video clip you wish to trim in QuickTime Player.

2. Choose Edit > Trim (Command-T). The trimming bar appears.

3. Drag the left or right edges to remove sections of the clip (**Figure 7.7**).

4. Click the Trim button or press Return to apply the trim.

Figure 7.7
Trimming a clip.

Drag edge of
trimmer bar.

5. Choose File > Save As to save your edited file.

> **tip** Here's a neat feature: Choose Edit > Select All Excluding Silence. Silent portions at the start or end of the clip are assumed to be moments when you were waiting for something to happen and are set for removal when you complete the trim.

tip　The trimmer bar only removes frames from the beginning and end of a clip. If you have two or more portions of a longer clip you want to save, duplicate the file in the Finder before opening it in QuickTime Player, then trim each copy to the section you want.

note　You cannot trim movies that include copy protection, such as movies you purchase through the iTunes Store.

Share media

Don't let the video sit neglected on your hard disk: send it to iTunes or upload it to your MobileMe Gallery or YouTube account.

1. Click the Share button in the controller (**Figure 7.8**).

Figure 7.8
Sharing from the controller.

2. Choose a destination from the pop-up menu that appears.

3. Enter information about the video and share it, based on the service:

   ▪ **iTunes.** Choose a size for the video: iPhone & iPod, Apple TV, or Computer; some options may not be available depending on the quality of the original video. Click Share to send it along.

- **MobileMe Gallery.** Enter a title and description, choose whether to include a version that will work for the iPhone and iPod touch, and set any access restrictions. Click Share to upload the video.

- **YouTube.** Enter your YouTube user name and password, then fill out data about the clip: Category, Title, Description, Tags, and Access. Click Next to view YouTube's terms of service, and then click Share.

Have Fun with Photo Booth

I initially thought Photo Booth was a nifty distraction, a way to highlight the fact that most Macs now include a built-in iSight camera. The application takes a photo or video and offers effects that you can apply and ways to share the finished pic. I didn't think people would use it a lot, but I was wrong. It's also a great first impression, being situated prominently on the Dock, for those who've just started using their first Mac.

note Don't believe me about Photo Booth's popularity? Check out the Mac Photo Booth group on Flickr, which boasts thousands of photos (www.flickr.com/groups/macphotobooth/).

Take a photo

To take a photo, click the Take Photo button in the middle of the toolbar (and smile!). Photo Booth counts down from 3 to 1 before taking the shot so you know when the image is captured (**Figure 7.9**, next page). As an extra touch, the screen goes white—not merely to replicate what we expect a camera to do, but to actually act as a flash and illuminate you. Photos appear in the tray at the bottom of the window.

tip To better replicate the old photo booth machines, click the second button on the toolbar, which makes Photo Booth capture four quick shots in succession when you click the Take Photo button.

Figure 7.9
*Taking a photo
in Photo Booth.*

The photo
countdown.

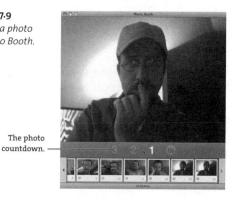

Apply effects

Photo Booth includes several visual effects to spice up (or completely weird out) your self-portraits.

1. Click the Effects button in the toolbar to view the available effects (**Figure 7.10**); the arrows to each side of the button display more effects.

2. Click the effect you want to use, then take your photo.

Figure 7.10
*Photo Booth
effects.*

Share photos

You can share your picture with others, or use it as a profile picture.

1. Select a photo in the tray at the bottom of the window.

2. Click one of the following buttons on the toolbar (**Figure 7.11**):

   - **Email.** The photo is sent to Mail (or your default email program) and attached to a new outgoing message. Enter a recipient and any personal note, and then send the message.

   - **iPhoto.** Add the picture to iPhoto.

   - **Account Picture.** The photo is assigned to your user account.

   - **Buddy Picture.** The photo is used in iChat as the image people who count you as a buddy will see in their buddy lists.

Figure 7.11
Sharing your photo.

tip   You can also drag a photo from the tray to the Desktop, a visible Finder window, or a document in another application.

Front Row

Apple sells the Apple TV, a device that lets you watch digital content on a high-definition television, but did you know that you can get nearly the same thing in Snow Leopard? Front Row uses much of the same software as the Apple TV to access the movies, music, TV shows, photos, and other media stored on your computer (**Figure 7.12**).

Figure 7.12
Front Row.

Front Row was designed to work with the Apple Remote, a diminutive remote control once included with new Macs but now available as a separate accessory. Press the Menu button to activate Front Row, or press Command-Esc. Then, Use the remote or arrow keys to navigate the Front Row interface, choosing which media to play. Press Menu again, or the Esc key, to exit Front Row.

tip If you own more than one Mac, you may be surprised to find your Apple Remote controlling all Macs in the immediate vicinity. To avoid this behavior, open the Security preference pane and click the General button. Next, click the Pair button to lock that remote to one computer.

8

Disks and Networking

No computer is an island, and you will frequently find yourself needing to move files from one computer to another. Mac OS X has many options for connecting storage devices to a Mac, and connecting to other computers over a network, whether a local network or the Internet. You can also easily burn a CD or DVD to move files around.

Snow Leopard treats all volumes (mounted drives) more or less the same, whether they directly attach to a port, connect over a local network or the Internet, or mount in a CD or DVD drive.

In this chapter, I cover how to attach and remove (or *mount* and *unmount*) drives, as well as how to manage drives over a network.

Connect a Storage Device

You'll run into two main kinds of storage devices: hard disk drives, which are enclosed in a case and attached via a cable; and memory drives (also called flash or thumb drives), which plug into a USB port.

External disk drives

Hard disk drives come in enclosures, cases that contain a power supply and interface ports along with the drive itself. (Some drives may not include cables, so double-check before you buy.)

Depending on your Mac, you may be able to connect drives with FireWire 400, FireWire 800, or USB 2.0 interfaces to your computer. Some Macs that are capable of running Snow Leopard lack any FireWire ports.

FireWire 400 and FireWire 800 are two different speeds of the same standard, and each has a different connector type. The faster and slower versions are compatible with each other, however. Modern USB drives come in just a single flavor, USB 2.0, which has a standard cable that works with all computers and drives.

tip You can purchase an adapter to let a FireWire 400 drive connect to a computer with just a FireWire 800 connector. However, it will still transfer data only at the slower speed.

Some hard drives have double, triple, or even quadruple interfaces that include USB 2.0, FireWire 400, FireWire 800, and/or eSATA, so you can choose the fastest available flavor.

Memory drives

A memory drive contains a small memory chip of the same sort used for digital camera storage. The drive has a connector, nearly always USB 2.0, that allows the drive to be used with a computer. Memory drives can be extremely tiny, and come in whimsical designs, such as molded plastic versions of popular sushi dishes.

Connect a drive

With a spare port available, plug the cable between an external hard drive and the computer, and then turn on the drive's power. Although you can power up a drive before the computer cable is plugged in, it's considered generally safer to connect the cable first.

A memory drive doesn't require power. Simply plug it into an available port, making sure it's securely inserted.

USB Hubbub

If all your USB ports are occupied, you can typically add a USB hub, which extends a single USB connection to allow two to four additional devices. Memory drives are sometimes built without enough space to allow them to be plugged into a USB port. A USB hub can give you better access, and you can locate it in a more convenient place than the back of the computer.

A *powered* USB hub is a better choice than a passive hub. A powered hub has to be plugged in separately to AC power, but it also allows the use of nearly any kind of USB device. Passive hubs, which are powered by the computer via the USB port, sometimes cannot pull enough juice to operate certain kinds of USB devices, such as cameras or even phone chargers.

Speaking of USB hubs, you may already have one: your keyboard, which contains USB ports. Also, many third-party monitors now include USB ports, turning the monitor into a hub as well.

Work with a mounted volume

When the drive is fully powered up, an icon representing the volume will appear on the Desktop and in the sidebar of Finder windows (**Figure 8.1**).

Figure 8.1
*A mounted
FireWire
hard drive.*

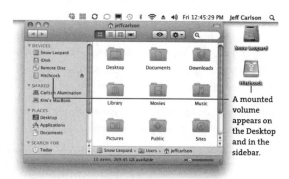

A mounted
volume
appears on
the Desktop
and in the
sidebar.

 note   Generally, a volume's icon indicates the type of drive or connection it uses, but sometimes a volume may appear with a generic icon.

Mounted volumes can be used just like a hard drive inside the computer. Memory drives and external hard drives can be used in precisely the same manner, too.

 tip   If you'd rather not clutter your Desktop, choose Finder > Preferences and, in the General pane, choose which items appear.

Unmount a Volume

When you've finished using a volume and want to remove it from the computer, it's critical that you eject it properly via software first. The Finder provides several options:

- Select the drive and choose File > Eject or press Command-E

- Drag the drive to the Dock's Trash icon, which changes to an Eject icon.

- Click the Eject icon to the right of a volume's name in the sidebar of a Finder window.

You don't want to detach the cable from your computer or power down an external drive, or pull out a memory drive, until you are sure that Mac OS X has finished several behind-the-scenes tasks for ejecting.

Snow Leopard adds a welcome way to be sure that you can remove the drive: The drive icon turns from solid to a grayed-back version while Mac OS X completes the removal process. Only when the drive disappears from the Desktop is it safe to disconnect the drive.

tip **Volumes are also safely unmounted when you shut down a Mac. When the shutdown process is complete, drives can be detached.**

tip **Another way to verify that a volume has been unmounted is to install HardwareGrowler, a component of Growl (growl.info) that displays an unobtrusive message when your hardware configuration changes.**

If you've opened any files from a mounted drive, Mac OS X won't let you eject the volume until the file is closed. Snow Leopard, unlike previous versions of Mac OS X, tells you which programs are tying up the volume (**Figure 8.2**).

Figure 8.2
Snow Leopard tells you what's preventing a volume from ejecting.

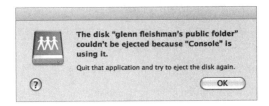

The disk "glenn fleishman's public folder" couldn't be ejected because "Console" is using it.

Quit that application and try to eject the disk again.

⑦   OK

note If you remove a drive before Snow Leopard is finished cleaning up hidden files and settings, the drive may not be mountable (Figure 8.3). Launch Disk Utility (found in the Utilities folder within the Applications folder) and run repair on the volume to try to fix it.

Figure 8.3
Snow Leopard chides you if you eject a disk too early.

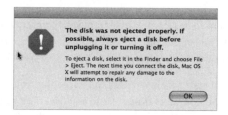

The disk was not ejected properly. If possible, always eject a disk before unplugging it or turning it off.

To eject a disk, select it in the Finder and choose File > Eject. The next time you connect the disk, Mac OS X will attempt to repair any damage to the information on the disk.

OK

Connect to a Networked Computer

If you own more than one computer or work with others on projects, files you need are often located somewhere other than on the machine in front of you. Networked file serving, in which a computer offers up access over a network to hard drives attached to it, lets you have all the documents you need at your fingertips.

note A server can share a single folder as if it were a complete volume to limit access to the rest of the files on a drive. This is useful when working with others who don't need (or who shouldn't have) full drive access.

Mount a networked volume

Computers on the network that have shared access enabled appear in two locations in the Finder (**Figure 8.4**).

- Choose Go > Network (Command-Shift-K).

- Look in the Shared heading in the sidebar of a Finder window.

Figure 8.4
Networked servers appear in the sidebar and Network window.

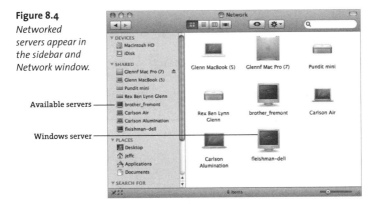

Available servers

Windows server

tip Computers running Mac OS X and other operating systems show up in the list of available computers; machines running Windows and other systems display a generic PC icon.

To mount a volume over the network, you must first connect to the server, then select the volume.

1. Double-click the server in the Network window, or select it from the Shared heading in the sidebar.

2. The window changes to show a connection in progress. The upper left displays "Connecting" until a connection is made. If a Guest account is set up on the computer you're connecting to, Mac OS X shows any folders available to guest users (**Figure 8.5**, next page). Stop here if this is all you need.

3. Click the Connect As button at the upper right. Enter the user name and password for the computer to which you are connecting.

note When you store a password, anyone using the same user account on the computer can mount the server without a password.

Figure 8.5
Connected to another Mac as Guest.

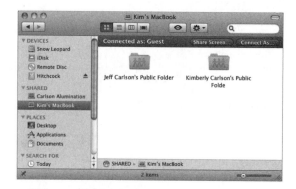

4. After you log in, the Finder window displays a list of available volumes, which can include both hard drives and folders. Double-click any volume to mount it on your computer.

 In the dialog asking for your password, enable the Remember This Password in My Keychain checkbox to bypass step 3 the next time you connect.

Mounted network volumes appear on the Desktop and in the sidebar, just as locally connected hard drives do. However, some routine operations, like opening and saving large files, will be slow if your network isn't set up using gigabit Ethernet connections.

 Want an easier way to mount a network volume? Select it on the Desktop and choose File > Make Alias (Command-L). The next time you want to mount that volume, simply double click the alias. If you haven't saved the password, you are prompted to enter it again.

Unmount a network volume

Unmount network volumes in the same way as a local drive.

- Select the drive and choose File > Eject, or press Command-E.
- Drag the drive to the Dock's Trash icon, which changes to an Eject icon.
- Click the Eject icon to the right of a server's name in the sidebar of a Finder window; this option ejects *all* mounted volumes belonging to that server.

View and control a network computer's screen

In Chapter 6, I demonstrated how to use iChat to share someone's screen. You can do the same thing with another Mac on your network without involving iChat.

1. In the Finder, connect to a network server and click the Share Screen button at the top of the window.

2. Enter your user name and password, if that information is not already stored. The other screen appears in a window on your computer **(Figure 8.6)**. When the pointer is within that window, you can control the computer remotely. When finished, just close the window.

Figure 8.6
Controlling a networked computer using screen sharing.

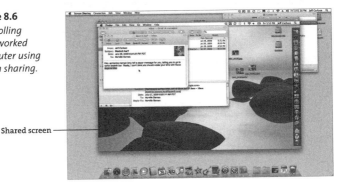

Shared screen

Back to My Mac

Back to My Mac lets you access computers you control beyond the local network you're on, just as if they appeared on the local network. This magic is carried out by using MobileMe to provide a kind of network glue.

On each computer for which you want to remote access enabled, open the MobileMe preference pane and enter your MobileMe user name and password. Click the Back to My Mac button and click Start to activate the service.

Computers reachable via Back to My Mac appear just like any other computer on your local network. You can connect to their files and also share their screens. However, network performance is restricted to the slower of the two connections.

Share Files from Your Mac

So far, this chapter has focused on connecting *to* another computer. But what if yours is the "other" computer? Snow Leopard provides a simple way to share files with other people, whether they're using Mac OS X, Windows, or other operating systems. Enable sharing by performing the following steps.

1. Open the Sharing preference pane (**Figure 8.7**).

2. Name your computer in the Computer Name field. (By default, Mac OS X inserts "*Your Name*'s Computer".)

3. Click the File Sharing checkbox in the Service menu at left to enable sharing.

Figure 8.7
The Sharing preference pane.

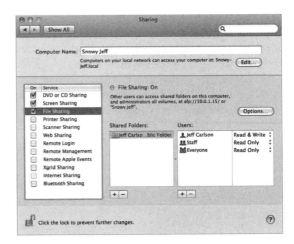

Choose one or more file sharing methods

Snow Leopard uses three standard file sharing methods. Click the Options button to enable or disable the following:

- **AFP (Apple Filing Protocol)**. AFP works with Mac OS X (and even earlier Mac OS) systems. It's rarely used except among Macs and certain networked hard drives. That said, AFP is enabled by default. If you're connecting only to Macs, you don't need to do anything else.

- **SMB (sometimes called Samba).** Windows default method for many years, and used commonly by other operating systems.

- **FTP (File Transfer Protocol).** FTP is an ancient Internet file-sharing type that's extremely insecure and should only be used with great care.

Specify what to share

You have complete control over which items are shared from the computer. Changes are applied immediately.

note You're not limited to sharing folders, even though the field is called Shared Folders. Hard disks and memory drives can also be shared to users with administrator privileges.

▪ To add items to share, click the Add (+) button beneath the Shared Folders. You can also drag a folder or drive from the Finder into the Shared Folders area. Shared items, and all nested folders within them, display a banner across the top of any Finder window (**Figure 8.8**).

Figure 8.8
A shared folder in the Finder.

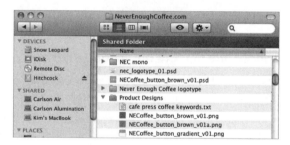

▪ To remove shared items, select the item and click the Remove (–) button.

Set who gets access

Snow Leopard lets you control who may access a given shared folder or drive, and what privileges they have to make changes or view the contents.

With an item selected in the Shared Folders list, those who have permission appear in the Users list at right. Each item is either a user with an account on the computer or a group of users. Several special system users and groups also appear:

- **Everyone**, which is any user on the system, including the Guest user.

- **Administrators**, which includes any user with the administrative option set for installing software or making other system configuration changes.

- **System Administrator**, a special extra-privileged user.

Guest Access

There's a dangerous combination of file sharing and guest access that you may need to guard against. In the Accounts preference pane, the Guest account is used to let people log in to Mac OS X without having privileged access and without leaving a trace (see Chapter 2).

However, it's also used to provide anonymous, password-free access to shared volumes that are marked as available to everyone. Guest access to shared folders is enabled by default.

Because AFP file sharing works over the Internet, if your Mac is directly connected using a publicly available address, and guest access is available, anything in the Public folder of any account on the machine is available, even if you'd intended it just for yourself or other users on a local network.

I recommend disabling guest access to folders:

1. In the Accounts preference pane, click the lock icon and enter an administrative account and password to make changes.

2. Select the Guest Account.

3. Disable the option to Allow guests to connect to shared folders.

Add users

If you're the only person who will access your Mac from another machine, your user account and privileges are already set up. Simply use your regular user name and password to gain access to your files.

You can also add users to a folder or drive by clicking the Add (+) button below the Users field, then choosing one of three methods (**Figure 8.9**):

Figure 8.9
Choose users who need access to a shared volume.

- Select the Users & Groups list item, choose a user or group in the right-hand pane, and click Select. These are user and groups that have already been created on the computer. Any users or groups already assigned to a shared item are grayed out.

- Click the Address Book item, select a person from your address book, and click Select. Choose a password for that person to use and enter it twice (to set and to verify it) in the dialog that appears. Doing so creates a sharing-only user account, which may only remotely log in to the computer to access files, and not log in from the computer itself.

- Click New Person and type a user name in the New Person dialog. Enter a password and verify it, then click Create Account. Select the person's name from the Users & Groups list and click Select to add them to the Users list.

note Even if you remove a user from the Sharing preference pane, the account still exists in the Accounts preference pane; go there if you want to delete the user from the computer entirely (see Chapter 2).

Choose what actions user and groups may perform

Each user or group may have one of three settings applied (**Figure 8.10**):

Figure 8.10
Each user or group may have separate permissions set for access.

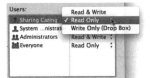

- **Read & Write.** This is the most common option, and allows the user or group to add, modify, or delete any item within the shared item.

- **Read Only.** This option limits the user or group to viewing a list of files and folders, and viewing the contents of any files. New files or folders may not be added, no changes may be made, and no item may be deleted.

- **Write Only (Drop Box).** If you need to allow someone to copy files to you, but not see anything else contained in a shared volume, this option lets them add items to a folder without seeing the contents of the folder.

A fourth option, No Access, is available only for the special Everyone group. You might want some users on a system to have access, but not every user.

Changes made to user and group rights are applied immediately.

 Changes made to file-sharing privileges also affect the rights of user accounts on the same machine when they're logged in at a different time than you.

 Snow Leopard adds the capability to share files even when the computer is asleep. In the Energy Saver preference pane, enable the

Wake for network access option. The computer still appears in the sidebar of Finder windows and the Network window, so other machines can connect to it. When that happens, the computer wakes up. This applies to sharing iTunes libraries, too, not just files.

Dropbox for File Synchronization

Copying files between computers via a network is useful when you need just a few files. However, you may want the same sets of files everywhere you work. Dropbox (www.getdropbox.com) automatically synchronizes the contents of a folder at two or more locations. Dropbox preserves older versions of files, and acts as an offsite backup as well. Apple's MobileMe offers a similar feature: If you're a member, open the MobileMe preference pane, click the iDisk button, and then enable the iDisk Sync feature by clicking the Start button. However, in my experience Dropbox has been more reliable and speedier. (I made extensive use of it while writing this book, automatically sharing screenshots from Snow Leopard test machines to my main computer.)

Dropbox also lets you share the contents of specific folders with other people and vice versa, allowing you to have the same set of files as project collaborators or family members. Another option is to create photo galleries from photos placed in folders.

You install a small software program that constantly monitors for changes in a folder (with as many nested folders as you want) on your computer, and receives notification of changes on other machines.

The service requires that you set up an account, which comes with 2 GB of storage at no cost. You can pay for more storage: 50 GB is $9.99 per month or $99 per year; 100 GB is $19.99 per month or $199 per year.

Burn a CD or DVD

You don't have to mount a drive directly or over a network to share files. Snow Leopard also supports the capability to write, or *burn*, them to a CD or DVD. The process is simple.

1. In the Finder, select items you want to burn. You can choose a folder, files, or any combination—even a mounted drive—as long as the contents will be able to fit on a single CD or DVD.

2. Choose File > Burn *[name* or *number of items]* to Disc.

3. Snow Leopard prompts you to insert a blank CD or DVD. The dialog box states how much storage is needed. Insert the disc.

4. Name the disc and, optionally, choose the speed at which it is burned (**Figure 8.11**).

Figure 8.11
Name the disc and choose a speed.

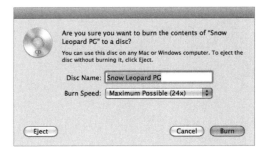

Are you sure you want to burn the contents of "Snow Leopard PG" to a disc?

You can use this disc on any Mac or Windows computer. To eject the disc without burning it, click Eject.

Disc Name: Snow Leopard PG

Burn Speed: Maximum Possible (24x)

Eject   Cancel   Burn

5. Click Burn. Mac OS X burns the disc, and then verifies it. When the process is complete, the disc appears on the desktop as a mounted volume.

tip Most modern optical drives can burn at the maximum rate. If you've had problems with disc burning failures, choose a slower rate, which is less likely to produce errors.

9

Printing

The Macintosh has printer toner in its veins, having popularized the first laser printers and started an era of desktop publishing. But printing is still a complicated affair: with many companies creating new models of printers, each with its own special features, printing a simple document becomes a tour of dissimilar dialogs and pop-up menus.

Snow Leopard benefits from decades of work to make the print process easier—as someone who's been there, you don't want to have to negotiate confusing options just to put ink or toner to paper on a deadline.

Add a Printer

Remember during the Snow Leopard installation when you had the option of excluding a large number of printer drivers to save space? One advantage to keeping those files intact is that Mac OS X can easily connect to almost any printer without requiring you to find and download a driver from the printer manufacturers' confusing Web sites. If this is your first time printing, or you need to connect to a different printer, the following steps will add a printer for you to use.

1. In any application that can print something, choose File > Print. The print dialog appears.

2. Click the Printer pop-up menu. Snow Leopard reports if any printers are already on the network; choose one to select it (**Figure 9.1**). Mac OS X communicates with the printer for a few seconds to determine its configuration. You can ignore the rest of these steps and proceed to printing the document.

   If, however, you don't see your printer in the list, choose Add Printer and continue reading.

Figure 9.1
Mac OS X lists connected printers or those on your network.

 tip You can also add a printer using the Print & Fax preference pane, but it's just as easy to choose File > Print and set up a printer from here.

3. In the Add Printer dialog, look for your printer in the Default pane; if it's there, select it.

Your printer may not automatically appear in the list if it uses a different style of connecting, such as over a network. If that's the case, do
one of the following:

- Click the IP button to view options for connecting to a printer that
  has its own network address (you may need to get this information
  from a network administrator, or consult the printer's documenta-
  tion). Select the type of communication from the Protocol pop-up
  menu, then enter the printer's address.

- Click the Windows button to connect to a printer via SMB/CIFS (the
  network protocol used by Windows to share printers).

tip **Normally, Mac OS X checks to see if it already has driver software for
the printer you select. If none is found, or you have troubles printing,
click the Print Using pop-up menu and choose Generic PostScript Printer or
Select Printer Software, and locate the printer model yourself from a list that
appears. Or, choose Other from the menu and locate software you may have
downloaded from the printer manufacturer's Web site.**

Print a Document

The printing process generally involves two stages. When you print a
document, either the default Mac OS X print dialog appears or a dialog
with custom options for that application appears.

After you set the options for that print job (such as deciding which pages
to print, for example), the data is sent to Snow Leopard's Print Queue,
which is an application created just for that printer; you'll see an icon for
the printer show up in the Dock. The Print Queue then sends the data to
the printer for printing.

Set Print Options

The steps detailed here represent an overview of print options you're likely to encounter. The software from which you're printing will have more information about specific features.

1. Choose File > Print. You'll probably see the simple version of the print dialog (**Figure 9.2**), which lets you choose a printer and a preset (see "Create a print preset," later in this chapter).

Figure 9.2
The basic print dialog.

If that's all the information you need, click the Print button to send the job to the Print Queue.

2. To reveal more print options, click the expansion triangle button to the right of the Printer pop-up menu.

3. Set various options for the job, such as the number of copies and which pages to print (**Figure 9.3**). Use the controls below the thumbnail at left to view a small preview of each page to be printed.

Figure 9.3
Advanced printing options.

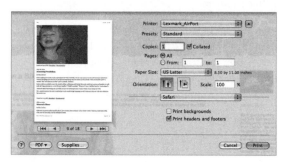

4. Click the unmarked pop-up menu below the standard options to reveal still more settings. Application-specific features appear when the program's name is selected from the menu; you'll also typically find access to the following panes (there are more, but these are ones you'll probably use most often) (**Figure 9.4**):

Figure 9.4
Advanced printing options.

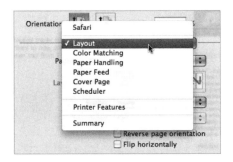

- **Layout.** Choose how many pages are to be printed on each sheet of paper, the direction of the page flow on the printout, whether a border is added, and other features related to how the print appears on paper.

- **Paper Feed.** If you're printing to paper that needs to be manually fed or from a specific print tray, choose Paper Feed from the pop-up menu.

- **Scheduler.** Control when a job will be printed.

tip If you have more than one printer set up, you can specify which one is the default printer. Open the Print & Fax preference pane and choose a printer from the Default Printer pop-up menu. Last Printer Used is the default.

Preview the job

To get a better idea of how the printout will appear, click the Preview button. (It may not appear if a thumbnail preview exists, as you can see in Figure 9.3.) Snow Leopard creates a PDF of the print job and opens it in the Preview application where you can review it. If the output looks acceptable, click the Print button at the bottom of the window; or, click Cancel to close the preview (**Figure 9.5**). You'll need to return to the application from which you were printing to make changes and print the job again.

Figure 9.5
*Preview a job
before printing.*

Print or cancel
the job

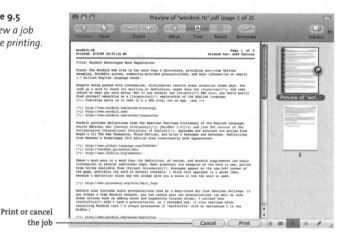

The Print Queue

When you send a print job to a printer, Mac OS X adds it to the Print Queue, an application created just for that printer. In the Print Queue window, you can view the jobs waiting to be printed, pause the printer, delete jobs before they're printed, or hold a job to be printed later (**Figure 9.6**).

Figure 9.6
The Print Queue.

Active print jobs —

Small print jobs process so quickly you may not catch them in the Print Queue before they're sent to the printer.

- **Pause the printer.** To put the brakes on all print jobs, click the Pause Printer button in the toolbar.

If the printer runs into a problem, such as a paper jam, the Print Queue may automatically pause the print jobs; click the Resume Printer button when the error has been fixed.

- **Delete a print job.** Select a print job in the list and click the Delete button to cancel that job. It's possible that a few pages may have printed before you cancelled it.

- **Hold a print job.** Click the Hold button to prevent a job from printing but keep it in the queue. This command is helpful if you're outputting a large job and need to print something short and quick before the job finishes.

Choose Jobs > Show Completed Jobs to view a list of print jobs that were processed through the queue.

tip In the Print Queue window, click the Supply Levels button to check the printer's levels of ink or toner. Clicking the Supplies button in the results window takes you to the online Apple Store and displays cartridges that are compatible with your printer—a helpful feature to locate the right part numbers if you choose not to order from Apple. (Not all printers support the Supply Levels feature.)

Create a print preset

If you often need to print documents with custom settings, such as with a border around each page, create a preset that applies the settings so you don't have to enable them each time.

1. Choose File > Print to open the Print dialog.

2. Apply the print settings you want.

3. From the Presets pop-up menu, choose Save As (**Figure 9.7**).

Figure 9.7
*Create a new
print preset.*

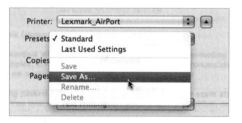

4. In the dialog that appears, enter a name for the preset and choose whether the preset applies to all printers recognized by your computer or to just that printer. Click OK.

   The next time you print, you can choose that preset from the Presets pop-up menu.

Print as a PDF

Mac OS X's print capability is useful even if you don't have a printer, or don't want to make a paper copy of something. Because the PDF format is deeply ingrained into the operating system, you can "print" a document to a PDF file. This feature is great for saving receipts of online orders or articles to read later when you may not have an Internet connection.

1. Choose File > Print to open the Print dialog.

2. Click the PDF button, which displays a pop-up menu (**Figure 9.8**).

Figure 9.8
Save a document as a PDF.

3. Choose Save as PDF.

4. Specify a location for the file, and add metadata such as a title, author, subject, and keywords to make the file easier to find later (such as using a Spotlight search). You can also specify security options: Set a password to open the PDF, to copy content, or to print the document.

5. Click Save to save the PDF to disk.

> **tip** Apparently, someone at Apple wanted an easy solution for saving online receipts. From the PDF pop-up menu, choose Save PDF to Web Receipts Folder. The first time you do this, Mac OS X creates a folder called Web Receipts in your Documents folder. This option saves you the trouble of specifying a location for each receipt.

10

Back Up Your Data

I wanted to title this chapter "MAKE BACKUPS!!", but didn't want to give my copyeditor a heart attack. Even without the all-caps and double exclamation points, I can't overstress the importance of setting up a good backup system.

If you think backups are merely a fine idea, and maybe you plan to copy a file or two to a CD once in awhile, let me propose this situation: You're sitting in front of your Mac, looking through your digital photos of when your kids were babies, or when you took that once-in-a-lifetime vacation. Then you start to hear a clicking noise, followed by your computer abruptly shutting down. When you restart it, the clicking noise has returned but nothing else.

Congratulations! Your hard disk has just suffered a head crash, where the mechanism that reads the data broke and started chopping into the disk surface—that clicking sound—destroying any chance of restoring your data. (Your only hope is to pay a couple thousand dollars to have a company such as DriveSavers (www.drivesaversdatarecovery.com) extract the data in a dust-free environment using forensic tools.)

I'm not exaggerating—it's happened to me. Hard disks fail, optical media degrades, disk directories become corrupted, laptops are stolen or are damaged. And your digital photos and other information are gone forever. The question is: What will you do to ensure your data remains safe? Backups, backups, backups.

The Pieces of a Good Backup System

Now that I've sufficiently scared you, I'm happy to point out that a good backup system is entirely possible. Snow Leopard includes Time Machine, a feature that automatically backs up your data every hour to an external hard drive or a network volume (including Apple's Time Capsule via Wi-Fi).

Notice I said "a good backup *system*." If your Mac's hard drive fails, you'll have the Time Machine backup, but what if that fails, too? To do this right (and you do want to do it right), a backup system needs a few key components:

- **An automatic backup.** The backup should happen with as little intervention from you as possible, to ensure that it gets done. Unless you're obsessively organized, it's easy to forget to connect a disk or run backup software on a regular schedule. Time Machine is one of the best features that was introduced in Mac OS X 10.5 Leopard, because it backs up your data in the background every hour.

- **A versioned backup.** Time Machine stores multiple copies of a file as it existed over time, so, for example, you can go back and retrieve the first draft of a document.

- **A bootable duplicate.** People focus on loss of data when something catastrophic happens, but don't forget about the loss of time. If your hard disk dies, you want to get up and running again without delay. In addition to a Time Machine backup, you want a recent complete duplicate of your hard disk that can be used to start up the computer (connected via FireWire or USB).

- **An offsite backup.** You can have multiple backups of your computer, but if a fire destroys your house, it will likely destroy all the copies of your data, too. Make sure your data is also backed up to another location, whether that involves copying important files to a MobileMe iDisk or other Internet-based backup system, or taking a duplicate hard drive to your office, a trusted friend's house, or a bank safety deposit box.

- **On-the-spot backups.** In addition to the elements above, you'll probably have smaller, temporary backups for important files that you're work-ing on. Those could be stored on CDs or DVDs, keychain memory drives, an iPod's hard disk, or other source.

My backup system

I know. It sounds daunting and complicated. But I'm no longer willing to risk the loss of my data, and I hope you feel the same way. If you don't want to be this comprehensive, or the cost is too great, at the very least use Time Machine on an external hard disk.

To give you an idea of what this looks like in a real-world setting, **Figure 10.1** (on the next page) illustrates my current backup system.

Figure 10.1

A diagram of my personal backup system.

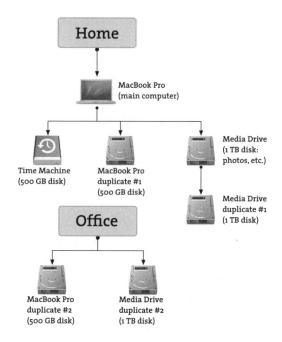

note The duplicate drives stored at my office and at home are rotated every few weeks, so I always have a recent duplicate at home and offsite.

note I've built my system based on the recommendations of my friend and colleague Joe Kissell, who's written extensively about the subject. I recommend his book *Real World Mac Maintenance and Backups*, as well as *Take Control of Mac OS X Backups*, an electronic book that I also edited (www. takecontrolbooks.com/backup-macosx).

Time Machine

Snow Leopard's Time Machine feature automatically performs a versioned backup of your entire hard disk, and updates it once every hour. If something happens—whether your Mac's hard drive dies or you accidentally delete a file—Time Machine can retrieve the data from the backup.

Set up Time Machine

Time Machine is enabled by default, making it easy to get started.

1. Connect an external hard disk to your computer. If this is the first time the disk has been mounted, a dialog appears asking if you'd like to use it as a Time Machine backup (**Figure 10.2**).

Figure 10.2
A polite inquiry when you attach a hard disk for the first time.

2. Click Use as Backup Disk to press the disk into service. If you click Don't Use, Time Machine ignores that drive as a backup source in the future (you can manually choose to use it later). After you click Use as Backup Disk, the Time Machine preference pane opens and the first backup begins (**Figure 10.3**).

Figure 10.3
The first backup copies all the files on your hard disk.

note The first backup could take quite a long time, depending on how much data is on your computer. Although you can still use your Mac while Time Machine is working, the initial backup may slow your system a bit. Start the process at night and let the copying happen while you sleep.

note You can use one external drive to back up multiple computers using Time Machine (provided you're willing to cart the drive to each machine). Each Mac gets its own directory on the backup disk. Just be sure to have plenty of free space to handle the needs of all the computers.

note It's also possible to use a network volume as a Time Machine backup. Mount the disk in the Finder (see Chapter 8 for more details), and set it as the backup disk in the Time Machine preference pane. You need to make sure the volume is mounted for ongoing backups.

How Much Storage for Time Machine?

When looking to buy an external hard disk, you may be tempted to save some money and buy a drive that roughly matches the capacity of your computer's hard disk. If you intend to use it with Time Machine, resist that urge and purchase the highest-capacity drive you can afford—at least 500 GB, but 1 TB or more is better.

When Time Machine makes a copy of a file that has changed, it holds onto the existing copy it made during the last backup. This approach is what enables you to reach back in time and grab the version from last Wednesday if you need it. Time Machine preserves hourly backups of files changed within the last 24 hours; daily backups for the past month; and weekly backups for all previous months.

All those copies take up space on the Time Machine disk, so you want a drive with plenty of capacity to store them. When the disk does fill up, Time Machine deletes the oldest backups to make room for new files.

Exclude items from the backup

You may not want to back up everything on your computer using Time Machine. For example, if you use virtualization software to run Windows, the data is stored in a multi-gigabyte disk image. Making one change to that environment flags the entire disk image as being modified, so Time Machine makes a new copy the next time it runs.

1. Open the Time Machine preferences.

2. Click the Options button.

3. Click the Add (+) button and choose the disk, folder, or file you wish to exclude (**Figure 10.4**), or simply drag the item from the Finder to the dialog. The Time Machine backup drive is automatically excluded.

4. Click Done to exit the dialog.

Figure 10.4
*Exclude items
from the backup.*

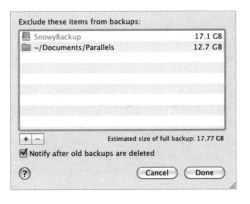

If you do exclude things from a Time Machine backup, make sure they're being backed up using some other method. You don't want to be reminded that you omitted something later when you need to get it back.

Perform a backup

Time Machine backs up files every hour, so there's no need to schedule a backup time. However, you may wish to manually trigger a backup, such as when you've finished a project or before upgrading software. To do so, go to the Time Machine icon in the menu bar and choose Back Up Now. (If you don't see the Time Machine icon, open the Time Machine preference pane and ensure that the Show Time Machine status in the menu bar option is enabled.)

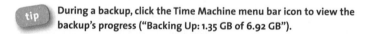 **If you do want to gain more control over when Time Machine backs up data, install TimeMachineScheduler, which lets you set an interval for the backup to occur and can skip a time range—forcing Time Machine to operate only at night, for example (www.klieme.com/TimeMachineScheduler.html).**

Pause a backup

If Time Machine is in the middle of a backup and you want to cancel it, choose Stop Backing Up from the Time Machine menu bar menu; or, click and hold the Time Machine icon in the Dock and choose the same thing. The next scheduled backup will occur on time.

tip **During a backup, click the Time Machine menu bar icon to view the backup's progress ("Backing Up: 1.35 GB of 6.92 GB").**

tip **If you interrupt a backup—such as by putting your computer to sleep or ejecting the backup disk—don't worry. Time Machine will pick up where it left off the next time the backup volume is available.**

Restore files from a backup

On a few occasions, Time Machine has saved my bacon by recovering files I'd accidentally deleted. Here's how to locate and restore old files.

1. In the Finder, do one of the following:

   ■ Open a window containing the folder where your desired file should appear.

   ■ Type the name of the file (or other search criteria) in the search field of a Finder window.

2. Click the Time Machine icon in the Dock, or choose Enter Time Machine from the Time Machine menu in the menu bar. Everything but the Finder window is replaced by a starry interface, and your mind is blown (**Figure 10.5**).

Figure 10.5
Time Machine activated.

Timeline

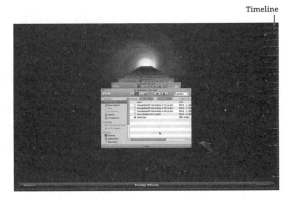

You can also browse your hard disk in this Finder window if you choose not to use the search field.

3. Click the top arrow to the right of the window to jump back to the most recent stored copy of the file (**Figure 10.6**). If you need an earlier version, click the arrow again, until you've located the one you want.

Figure 10.6
*Locating a
deleted file.*

> **tip** Select a file and press the spacebar to activate Quick Look on any file to make sure you're getting the right one.

4. Select the file and click the Restore button. The file is copied from the backup drive to its original location, and you're returned to the Finder.

> **tip** Although the backup volume is mounted right there on your desktop, don't go poking through it to find a file—you're much better off letting Time Machine do the locating for you.

Restore data from applications

Time Machine isn't just a tool to use in the Finder. Some applications, such as Mail and iPhoto, are savvy about Time Machine and enable you to restore individual messages or records. When you're in the application, click the Time Machine icon in the Dock to enter the Time Machine environment and follow the instructions above.

Restore an entire drive

In the event that something catastrophic happens (most likely a hard drive failure) and you need to recover your entire drive's worth of data, you can do it from the Time Machine backup.

1. Start your computer from the Mac OS X installation disc: Insert the disc and hold down the C key.

2. Select your language in the first screen of the Snow Leopard installer.

3. Choose Utilities > Restore System From Backup.

4. After reading the warning that restoring erases everything currently on your disk, select your Time Machine backup drive.

5. Select one of the full Time Machine backups listed in the next window.

> **tip** **If your original data was destroyed, you probably want the most recent full backup. However, if your Mac became unstable after installing some software, or you think some other event could have corrupted the data, choose an earlier backup from the list.**

6. Select the destination disk (your Mac's internal hard disk, most likely) and click the Restore button.

Time Capsule

If you use a laptop or have several Macs in your house, it may not be convenient to attach an external hard drive to each one. (My wife's MacBook stays in the living room, and she doesn't want a hard drive and its associated cables as table decoration.) Apple's Time Capsule device is a wireless AirPort base station with a built-in hard disk set up to use Time Machine (www.apple.com/timecapsule/).

Set up the Time Capsule for Time Machine

Use AirPort Utility to configure the Time Capsule as a base station, including routing your Internet connection. Once it's set up, do the following:

1. In the Time Machine preference pane, click the Select Backup Disk button.

2. Choose the Time Capsule disk and click Use for Backup.

3. Enter the password you set up for the Time Capsule. The backup commences.

tip **Connect your Mac to the Time Capsule via Ethernet for the initial backup, since copying files over a wireless network is slower than Ethernet.**

After the first backup, Time Machine works the same with the Time Capsule as it does with a local disk.

Archive the Time Capsule disk

In the event the Time Capsule's hard disk fails or the device becomes inoperable, it's good to have a backup of your Time Machine data. Apple included the option of making an archive to a hard drive connected to the Time Capsule via USB. Do the following.

1. Connect a hard drive to the Time Capsule.

2. Open AirPort Utility (located in the Utilities folder).

3. Connect to the Time Capsule by double-clicking it in the sidebar.

4. Click the Disks button; the Time Capsule's hard disk and the external disk appear in the list within the Disks pane (**Figure 10.7**).

Figure 10.7
*The Time
Capsule's disks in
AirPort Utility.*

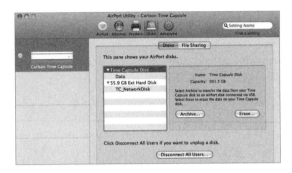

5. Select the Time Capsule and then click the Archive button.

6. Choose the name of the attached disk in the next dialog and click
   Archive.

7. After reading the disclaimer (the external disk is unavailable while
   archiving), click the Archive button. The status of the operation
   appears in the Disks pane.

Make a Duplicate

As I mentioned earlier, having a duplicate of your hard disk means you
can get your computer running again quickly. However, making a duplicate is more involved than merely copying your files from one disk to
another in the Finder (an approach that worked in the Mac OS 9 days).
Mac OS X hides many system files from view, so the best action to take
now is to use a program such as SuperDuper (www.shirt-pocket.com) or
CarbonCopyCloner (www.bombich.com). Both applications copy everything and set up the external disk so that you can start up your computer
from it.

Make a duplicate using SuperDuper

SuperDuper and CarbonCopyCloner operate similarly enough that I'm going to go through the steps of setting up a duplicate in SuperDuper, since that's what I currently use.

1. Attach and mount an external hard disk.

> **tip** SuperDuper can erase the backup drive during its progress, so you don't need to format it beforehand.

2. Launch SuperDuper.

3. Choose your Mac's hard disk from the first Copy pop-up menu, then choose the backup drive from the "to" pop-up menu (**Figure 10.8**).

Figure 10.8
SuperDuper.

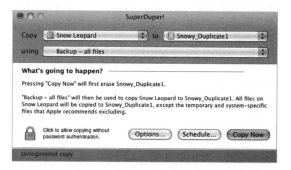

4. Choose Backup - all files from the "using" pop-up menu. SuperDuper provides other options, such as copying only changed files, but for this example you want to make a complete duplicate of the drive.

5. Click Copy Now to start the process. Enter your administrator password and then click the Copy button in the dialog confirming your action. The backup commences.

The Amazing Hard Disk Toaster

With all my talk of backing up to external hard disks and making duplicates, you're probably envisioning a nightmare of cables and power adapters. That doesn't have to be the case.

Instead of buying external drives that include an enclosure, ports, and an always-bulky power supply, I bought a "toaster": one device into which you insert bare SATA hard drives. The one I purchased, a NewerTech Voyager Q (newertech.com/products/voyager_index.php) sports an array of ports to connect to the computer: two FireWire 800, one FireWire 400, one USB 2.0, and one eSATA. When you insert either a 3.5-inch or 2.5-inch hard drive (just the drive itself, **Figure 10.9**) and power the device, the disk mounts on your desktop.

It's not something you'd want to use as a permanent disk solution, since the electronics on the bottom of the hard drive are exposed, but it's great for making duplicates. Better yet, the bare drives are much less expensive than drives that come in enclosures and are easy to transport offsite; consider buying a few anti-static protective cases, such as those offered by WiebeTech (www.wiebetech.com/products/cases.php).

Figure 10.9
NewerTech Voyager Q "toaster" dock, with a drive.

Back Up Files Online

If you have a speedy broadband Internet connection, you can take advantage of another backup option: copy files to a remote server. Depending on the service, files are encrypted and stored on a computer outside your house (and most likely outside your state). When you need to recover a lost file, you connect to your stored backup—either via the Web or using the backup software—and copy the file back to your computer. Online backups let you maintain an offsite backup without needing to rotate hard disks.

Automated backups

A growing number of companies, such as Mozy (mozy.com) and Crash-Plan (www.crashplan.com), offer online backup services at various rates. MozyHome, for example, lets you store up to 2 GB of data for free (noncommercial use), or an unlimited amount of data for $4.95 per month. CrashPlan take a slightly different approach, giving you the option of copying an unlimited amount of data to a friend's computer or another computer you own (such as one at work, also running CrashPlan). Or, you can back up to CrashPlan Central, a data storage location run by the company; it costs $0.10 per gigabyte per month, with a $5.00 minimum charge. Both companies also offer pro services that cost more.

However, Internet speeds are still far too slow (especially in the United States) to back up an entire hard disk—it could take weeks. The best approach is to choose which data you wish to copy offsite (**Figure 10.10**) and continue to rely on alternate backup solutions.

note **When determining if you want to use an online backup service, keep in mind that the upstream bandwidth on your Internet service is probably far slower than what you enjoy downstream. My cable Internet service is**

advertised as having up to 15 Mbps (megabits per second) downstream but only 3 Mbps upstream (which itself is more than many packages).

Figure 10.10
Choosing data to back up in MozyHome.

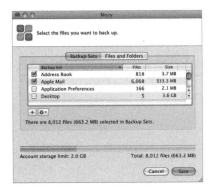

Back up essential files

An automated backup is great for peace of mind, but I often sleep better at night after making online copies of current projects. It's a manual process, but that's okay: I simply drag a folder to my MobileMe iDisk or to my Dropbox folder (see the sidebar "Dropbox for File Synchronization" in Chapter 8)—or to both, if I'm feeling particularly paranoid about losing some data, such as at the end of a big project.

11

Keep Your Mac Secure

Apple made smart decisions from the first release of Mac OS X to prevent a host of security problems from affecting its operating system. No computer is completely immune to problems such as viruses and attacks, but Snow Leopard is pretty solid.

Not to sound alarmist, but that doesn't mean your data is completely safe. Miscreants who want to compromise your computer for their own purposes, steal your information to impersonate you digitally, or simply mess up your machine are always inventing new ways to break in.

To ensure the safety of your data and your use of the Internet, this chapter explains how to take full advantage of Snow Leopard's security features.

Passwords

Passwords are the unfortunate backbone of security. They're unfortunate because your ability to protect something, such as access to your computer and its files, is limited to how well you choose a password.

tip If you ever receive email or a phone call that purports to be from a firm you deal with in which someone asks for your password, it's nearly guaranteed to be a scam. If they're legitimate, there will be some mechanism for you to reset your password without divulging any sensitive information. Never give out your password.

Choose a strong password

Good passwords share the following traits:

- Are a mix of letters, numbers, and punctuation.

- Contain no words found in dictionaries in common languages.

- Do not substitute 3 for e, o (zero) for the letter o, or ! for the numeral 1. (These common substitutions are trivial to overcome by crackers.)

- Omit names, especially family names (that includes pet names!).

- Avoid numbers associated with your or family members' birthdays.

This can be a lot to remember. Fortunately, Apple offers built-in help to create a strong password.

Create a password using Password Assistant

Snow Leopard includes a password generator that can create passwords for you that are as strong as you like. However, it's a little hard to find.

1. Launch the Keychain Access application, located in the Utilities folder (which is in the Applications folder).

2. Select File > New Password Item.

3. In the dialog that appears, click the key icon to the right of the Password field ( ). The Password Assistant appears with a password in the Suggestion field (**Figure 11.1**).

Figure 11.1
The Password Assistant helps you create strong passwords.

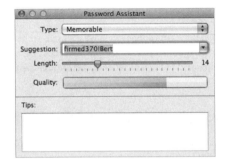

4. Choose a type of password to be generated from the Type pop-up menu, such as Memorable, which includes words in your language. If a so-called memorable password is long enough, Password Assistant includes enough other characters to make the password secure.

   You can also type your own password into the Suggestion field.

5. Click the Suggestion field's pop-up menu to see more choices. You can also drag the Length slider to change the number of characters in the password, thereby increasing its strength.

   The assistant shows how good or poor a password is through the Quality bar. Weak passwords score a short bar in red. Good passwords earn a longer bar in green.

tip Password Assistant is also available in other places in Snow Leopard, including the Accounts preference pane when creating new accounts.

tip   Always create the strongest password you can tolerate for user
accounts in Mac OS X. With a user account's password in hand, anyone who can walk up to your computer, connect over a local network (such as at a Wi-Fi hot spot), or reach you remotely over the Internet can access files or worse on your computer. With a user account that has administrative access, someone can install malicious software.

tip   The developers at codepoetry have a simple program, called Password
Assistant, that lets you launch the Mac OS X Password Assistant as a freestanding application (www.codepoetry.net/products/passwordassistant).

Store Secure Data in Your Keychain

Your sensitive data shouldn't be left out for all to see. This includes pass-words, but it also includes notes to yourself with your credit card number in it or other private information you may want to access.

Mac OS X stores passwords and other security items, such as digital certificates, in keychains, which Snow Leopard keeps encrypted using your account password as the key. Whenever you're prompted by a program or service to store a password in the keychain, a new entry is added or an existing one is modified.

note   To change passwords associated with programs or services (such as
AirPort Utility or Screen Sharing), don't make the changes within Keychain Access. Instead use the program in which the password was created.

Save Web site passwords

Just as you don't want to expose your private information, you also don't want to use the same password for every Web site that requires login information (such as your bank and online stores). Safari and many other

Web browsers store that information in the keychain. Do the following when signing in to a secure Web site for the first time—I'm using Safari as the example browser here.

> **note** Firefox stores passwords for Web sites in its own database, not in a Mac OS X keychain. You can access them in Firefox's preferences on the Security pane; click the Saved Passwords button.

1. Load a Web site with a login form.

2. Enter your name and password, and press Return or click the Log In button (the name of the button varies; it's whatever sends the data).

   Safari asks if you'd like to save the password for use later (**Figure 11.2**).

Figure 11.2
*Save a Web
site password.*

3. Click Yes to save the information. If you'd prefer to always enter the password manually, click Never for this Website. Or, click Not Now to decide later.

   The password information is saved in the keychain and the Web site continues to load.

The next time you visit that site, Safari automatically fills in the user name and password fields; the password characters are exchanged for bullet characters to hide the contents from peering eyes. You can log in without looking up the information.

Look up passwords in your keychain

The problem with having multiple passwords, of course, is that it's difficult to remember them all, especially ones that were generated by the Password Assistant. As long as you remember your Mac OS X user account password, you can look up the others.

1. Launch Keychain Access and select the "login" keychain from the list at left.

2. Locate the login you're looking for in the main list; you may want to type part of the site's name into the search field in the toolbar.

3. Double-click the login to view details about it.

4. By default, the password is not shown; click the Show password checkbox and enter your user account password to make it visible (**Figure 11.3**).

Figure 11.3
View a password in the keychain.

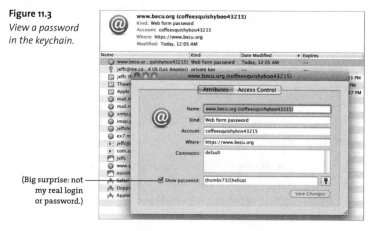

(Big surprise: not my real login or password.)

Create secure notes

Keychain Access manages items in the keychain, which lets you view passwords you've stored and create secure notes that require your password to decrypt. Do the following to create a secure note:

1. Launch Keychain Access.

2. Select File > New Secure Note Item.

3. Enter a title and text for your note, and then click Add (**Figure 11.4**). The note is now stored securely, requiring your user account password to access.

Figure 11.4

Create a secure note.

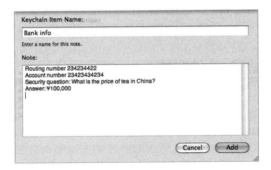

To access the contents, follow these steps.

1. In Keychain Access, double-click the secure note.

2. Check the Show Note box.

3. Enter your user account password (**Figure 11.5**, next page). Click Always Allow to bypass entering the password again for this item. Click Allow to show the note just this one time.

Figure 11.5

Retrieve the contents of a secure note.

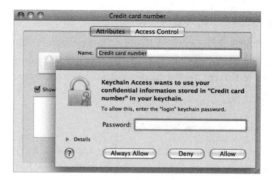

Other Secure Data Storage Options

Beyond Keychain Access, I recommend two other programs to store passwords, logins, and other data securely.

- 1Password (agilewebsolutions.com/products/1Password) lets you create and manage passwords in Web browsers with a toolbar and menu for Firefox, Safari, and others. It also stores secure notes, and can synchronize among your computers and with either a regular or pro version for the iPhone or iPod touch.

- Yojimbo (www.barebones.com/products/Yojimbo/) stores all manner of items with varying security options, including notes, passwords, serial numbers, PDFs, and Web archives.

Don't Use FileVault

When talking about Mac OS X security, you'd think one of the items high on the list would be FileVault, a way to automatically protect all the data in your home folder. When FileVault was introduced in Mac OS X 10.3 Panther, I thought the same thing. However, the feature has too many shortcomings to be of real use, even after several years of development, and I recommend keeping it turned off.

The idea is that FileVault encrypts the entire contents of your home folder, where you're most likely (and encouraged) to store all your documents and important information. However, FileVault can't *exclude* any items, so all your media—songs, podcasts, videos, and photos, all of which happen to take up enormous amounts of hard disk space—are encrypted.

The encryption also makes it difficult to back up your home folder. If you're logged in, then protection is off, and files can be backed up. But if another user is logged in or you use a networked backup system, FileVault makes your home folder into one giant encrypted file. Any change you make to any of the data when logged in results in the entire file getting backed up, which translates into gigabytes of wasted storage. If you're using Time Machine for backups, it's worse: nothing in the home folder is backed up until you log out.

A better approach is to create an encrypted disk image using Apple's Disk Utility, and store confidential or private files there. (Follow this link for instructions: http://db.tidbits.com/article/9673.)

You can also go whole hog and encrypt your entire hard disk using PGP's Whole Disk Encryption software (na.store.pgp.com/whole_ disk_encryption_mac.html). When the computer is powered off, none of the data on your disk is accessible.

I want to like FileVault, I really do, but it's too much of a blunt instrument to be used effectively.

Enable the Firewall

Software developers stole the term *firewall* from the building industry, where construction techniques prevent a fire from passing from one compartment to another. A computer firewall keeps the bad stuff out, separating your computer from the network it's on, or the Internet.

Mac OS X includes a modest firewall that's part of a good strategy for protecting your computer from outside influences. Firewall settings are found in the Security preference pane in the Firewall tab.

note Apple's firewall covers incoming connections to applications only, and only in a limited fashion. More full-featured firewalls and application monitors can monitor incoming requests to services and programs, restrict those requests by address or type, and even let you know when programs are trying to reach out to the Internet. Check out DoorStop X Firewall (www.opendoor.com/DoorStop/) and Little Snitch (www.obdev.at/products/littlesnitch/).

Activate the firewall

Apple simplified the firewall in Snow Leopard, displaying just a Start button that, when pressed, enables the feature.

1. Open the Security preference pane and click the Firewall button.

   If the Start button is grayed out, click the lock icon and provide your user account password.

2. Click Start to activate the firewall.

Control access to applications

With the firewall turned on, you'll be asked when launching an application whether you want to allow it to accept incoming connections; for instance, iPhoto with library sharing enabled lets others browse pictures over the network. Click Allow to give it the all-clear approval (**Figure 11.6**).

Figure 11.6
The firewall
doing its job.

For a few more options, click the Advanced button (**Figure 11.7**).

- **Block all incoming connections.** This option prevents any inbound access except for a few limited services, including Back to My Mac.

- **Individual service settings.** Each service that allows incoming access appears in the main list above the gray dividing line. Disable access to services by disabling them in the Sharing preference pane.

- **Individual applications.** Turn access on or off for any application using the pop-up menu next to the program. You can also manually configure applications by clicking the Add (+) or Remove (–) buttons.

Figure 11.7
Set advanced
options for
the firewall.

Choose to allow or —
block connections
to a given program.

☐ Block all incoming connections
Blocks all incoming connections except those required for basic Internet services,
such as DHCP, Bonjour, and IPSec.

DVD or CD Sharing	⊜ Allow incoming connections
File Sharing (AFP)	⊜ Allow incoming connections
Screen Sharing	⊜ Allow incoming connections
iPhoto	✓ ⊜ Allow incoming connections
	● Block incoming connections

+ −

☑ Automatically allow signed software to receive incoming connections
Allows software signed by a valid certificate authority to provide services accessed
from the network.

☐ Enable stealth mode
Don't respond to or acknowledge attempts to access this computer from the network
by test applications using ICMP, such as Ping.

⊙   (Cancel) (OK)

- **Automatically allow signed...** lets the firewall pass programs that have been verified by a third party to be legitimate. This includes software from Apple.

- **Enable stealth mode.** This option makes your computer ignore requests that are designed to check for the existence of a computer at a given address and which are often meant as probes for malicious intent.

General Security Precautions

You can quickly increase your security quotient through a few simple steps.

- **Apply security updates.** This counts both for Apple's updates, found in Apple > Software Update, and which you're routinely notified of, but also updates for programs you routinely use. Most software automatically offers updates.

- **Enable Use secure virtual memory** in the Security preference pane's General options. This setting prevents private data from being stored and sometimes left on your hard drive when your RAM (memory) is full. Someone with access to the computer could extract vital data.

- **Turn on Require Password after sleep or screen saver begins,** also in the Security preference pane. This prevents easy access to your machine if left alone or behind, and is especially recommended for laptops.

Anti-Virus Software

If you've come to the Mac from a Windows background, you know that any Windows-based PC needs a good anti-virus package. On the Mac, however, it's not needed. Seriously.

As of this writing, there are currently no active, dangerous viruses for the Mac. Part of that is due to security steps Apple has taken when engineering Mac OS X (Microsoft's Windows Vista and Windows 7 also feature a drastically improved security architecture). But the Mac so far has also been a smaller, more difficult target; it's much easier for malcontents to write viruses targeting Windows XP, which ensures greater infection.

The Mac isn't immune to viruses, of course, but so far there hasn't been a need to spend money and your computer's processing cycles toward anti-virus software. The best thing you can do right now is to stay abreast of security updates and follow news outlets such as TidBITS (tidbits.com, where I'm an editor).

Surf Safely

The most dangerous program on your computer is your Web browser. Criminals worldwide would like nothing better than to have you visit malicious sites, download and install software you shouldn't, and fool you into thinking you're at your bank's Web site instead of their bogus stand-in. Don't be fooled.

While Mac OS X is resistant to common strategies that worked against Windows XP, the weakest link in your computer's security is, I'm afraid to say, you—and ne'er-do-wells know this. But you can easily avoid their lures by adhering to the following advice and using common sense.

Use a modern Web browser and keep it up to date

All the modern browsers for Mac OS X are currently considered secure when all the security patches and updates have been installed. Some browsers release updates every few weeks.

If you're using a browser that's a year or two old, or if you haven't bothered to get the latest update, upgrade now (see Chapter 4 for details on upgrading software).

Don't install unfamiliar software

This may go without saying, but if a site offers you software with which you're unfamiliar, especially if you can't find reviews online—don't do it. (This is true for any software that someone emails you, too.)

Mac OS X hasn't been plagued with software that installs itself or runs without user action, but proof-of-concept programs have been shown to exist. Evildoers rely on convincing you to launch and install software that causes harm.

Don't install custom video-player software

Several Mac attacks have centered on software that you allegedly need to install in order to view video files in some format that QuickTime doesn't support. Don't install it.

Disable the Open "safe" files option in Safari

If you use Safari, immediately open Safari's preferences and, in the General pane, disable the option labeled Open "safe" files after down-loading (**Figure 11.8**). While Apple intended this feature to enhance security by disabling the automatic opening of "unsafe" files, exploits in the past have been based on hiding bad code in media and other file types.

Figure 11.8
The safe option isn't the smart option.

☑ Open "safe" files after downloading
"Safe" files include movies, pictures, sounds, PDF and text documents, and disk images and other archives.

Look for a green bar or highlighting for secure sites

A secure Web site shows a lock icon somewhere in the browser to indicate that your browser and the Web server have created an encrypted connection, and that the Web server is at the Internet address it claims. But many sites have gone one step farther by employing Extended Validation (EV) secure certificates. An EV certificate is supposed to ensure that whatever firm set up the Web site has been vetted even further to validate its identity.

The EV status is shown by a green bar or green highlighting in the Location field, where the URL appears (**Figure 11.9**). Most banks, credit unions, lending institutions, and credit card companies have paid slightly higher fees for this identity confirmation to reassure customers.

Figure 11.9
The EV indicator in Safari 4 (top) and in Firefox 3.5 (bottom). Click the bar for more details on the site's identity.

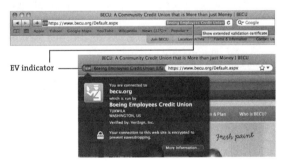

If you visit a site of this kind and it lacks the green marker, but you've seen it there before, something's definitely wrong. And if a financial institution you deal with hasn't seen fit to go green, you should let them know that it matters.

Use OpenDNS to detect phishing sites

Phishing is the art of convincing you to visit a Web site that purports to be one you know but is actually run by a scammer. Phishing sites can be quite realistic, and often employ domain names and other masking techniques that defuse your anxiety.

Fortunately, several firms have assembled and constantly update lists of Web pages and sites that are used as part of phishing attacks. They also often mark malicious sites that contain malware, or software designed to attack your computer when visiting the site (so far, this is largely a Windows problem).

You can use one list of phishing sites to protect your surfing by changing a network setting to point to OpenDNS (opendns.com), a free provider of domain name service (DNS). (DNS is an Internet method of converting a human readable name, like peachpit.com, into a numerical Internet address.) OpenDNS uses this list to identify and then block your access to these sites (**Figure 11.10**).

Figure 11.10
OpenDNS blocks and explains phishing sites.

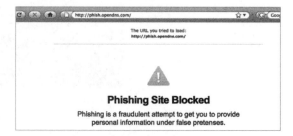

To configure OpenDNS to provide domain lookups for your machine:

1. In the Network preferences pane, select your network connection—
   the one with a green dot next to it—such as Ethernet or AirPort.

2. Click the Advanced button.

3. Click the DNS button at the top.

4. Under the DNS Servers area, click the Add (+) button and enter
   208.67.222.222. Then, click the Add (+) button again, and enter
   208.67.220.220. (You add two addresses for redundancy in case one
   server happens to be unavailable.)

5. Click OK.

6. Click Apply.

You can also set OpenDNS for an entire network if you use a gateway or
base station (such as an AirPort Extreme) to provide network addresses
via DHCP. In that device's setup program, enter the DNS server values
above.

Network Safely with Wi-Fi

The last piece of the personal security puzzle is protecting your computer
when connecting to a network via Wi-Fi wireless networking. Wi-Fi is
a weak link because signals travel through the air, and anyone with
another computer and free software can intercept and view your data if
it's not secured.

note **Ethernet-connected computers and broadband networks are generally
considered safe. Ethernet requires physical access—someone in your
house or office—to break into. Broadband networks are generally well secured
and monitored at the various network buildings through which data passes.**

Use a VPN at hot spots

If you use your Mac at a Wi-Fi hot spot, such as a café, you need to secure your connection so data isn't sent without protection between your computer and the hot spot's Internet connection. A virtual private network (VPN) connection offers this option. VPNs create an encrypted tunnel between your computer and a server somewhere else on the Internet. This tunnel can't be penetrated with any known cracking software. Most corporations require roaming workers to use a VPN.

Individuals can "rent" a VPN connection from several firms. You can pay for access to publicVPN ($69.95 per year or $6.95 per month, publicvpn. com) and WiTopia ($39.95 to $69.95 per year, www.witopia.net).

Use Wi-Fi encryption

On your own network or one you manage, enable encryption and use a passphrase. For Apple's Wi-Fi base stations, either use the setup assistant when configuring the base station, or follow these steps:

1. Launch AirPort Utility from the Utilities folder.

2. Select your base station in the list at left, and click Manual Setup.

3. Select the AirPort view and click the Wireless button.

4. From the Wireless Security pop-up menu, select WPA/WPA2 Personal if you have any Macs or Windows systems from 2004 or before, or WPA2 Personal if all computers were made in 2004 or later.

5. Enter a password in the Wireless Password field, and re-enter it in the Verify Password field.

6. Click Update and wait for the base station to restart.

 The same password will work with Windows, iPhone, and all other devices with Wi-Fi sold in 2004 or later.

12

Troubleshooting

With Apple's emphasis on making the Mac easy to use, it's easy to forget that under the crisp colors and soft drop shadows lies a complex bed of code that runs the show. No software is ever perfect, and although Apple has focused on improving performance and stability in Snow Leopard, bugs and other issues are sure to crop up.

This chapter is an introduction to troubleshooting problems, offering some general advice to help you locate and solve issues that might arise. I also provide specifics about repairing disk directory corruption, dealing with applications that frequently crash or refuse to operate, and working through network and connectivity issues.

General Troubleshooting

When something goes wrong on your Mac, it's often not clear what is causing the problem. The following is a list of general suggestions intended to narrow down the cause of the problem.

■ **Restart the computer.** Applications can exhibit strange behavior when there isn't enough memory available for them to operate, which can happen if you've been running lots of applications for days or weeks. Or, perhaps a buggy program is interfering with other processes. Restarting the computer clears the caches and resets the environment.

■ **Log in as a different user.** Remember in Chapter 2 when I recommended creating a test user account? Log out of your current account, then log in to the test one and see if the problem persists. If it's gone, then the culprit is some software running (most likely in the background) in your main user account. See "Startup Modes," later in this chapter to log in with startup items disabled.

■ **Check cables and connections.** "Of course, *that* couldn't be it," I've said to myself on more than one occasion. And yet, after checking my hard disk for errors, running utilities, and restarting the computer, the problem has sometimes been a video or network cable that wasn't snug, or a bad FireWire or USB cable. Verify that all your connectors are tight. If the problem is reading an external disk or connecting to a network, try a different cable.

■ **Look online for more information.** It's possible other people are experiencing the same problem as you. Apple's support forums (discussions. apple.com) are a good place to start, as is a general Google search.

tip My colleague Adam Engst wrote an article that presents a methodical approach to diagnosing computer problems. See "TidBITS Trouble-shooting Primer," Part 1 (db.tidbits.com/article/6968) and Part 2 (db.tidbits.com/article/6975).

Troubleshoot Disk-Related Issues

Mac OS X tracks the attributes of hundreds of thousands of files—not just where they're located on disk but also what permissions apply to each one, how they interact with other files, and more. It does this efficiently, but sometimes the data can become corrupted by a bad installer, a buggy program, or, I'm convinced, gremlins.

Verify disk structure

Mac OS X maintains a directory of your disk's file structure, which can get corrupted. The files themselves are usually perfectly fine, but the system has trouble locating them, which could lead to overwritten files if things get particularly bad. But it won't get that far, right? Because now you know what to do:

1. Launch Disk Utility, which is located in the Utilities folder within the Applications folder (or, in the Finder, choose Go > Utilities or press Command-Shift-U).

2. Select a volume in the left-hand pane and click the First Aid button at the top of the screen.

3. Click the Verify Disk button. A dialog informs you that the computer may be slow during the verification process; click Verify Disk to continue. Disk Utility scans the disk's directory (**Figure 12.1**, next page) and flags any problems.

4. If errors are found, Disk Utility can repair them, but it depends on which disk you're checking. The Repair Disk button is disabled if you're analyzing the startup disk. See the sidebar "Repairing the Startup Disk" in Chapter 2 for instructions on how to repair the disk using the Snow Leopard install disc. If you've verified a non-startup disk, click Repair Disk to fix the errors.

Figure 12.1

*Disk Utility
verifying a disk.*

5. After performing the repair, click Verify Disk again to make sure there are no other problems. If everything comes up green, you can quit Disk Utility.

tip Sometimes directory corruption is too severe for Disk Utility to repair. In that case, turn to Alsoft's DiskWarrior (alsoft.com), which succeeds where many other disk utilities fail.

Repair permissions

Every file on your hard disk is tagged with permissions that limit what actions can be performed, such as whether a file can be edited or not and which user accounts can act on it. Click Repair Disk Permissions in the First Aid pane of Disk Utility. Repairing permissions was once thought to be a general fix for any weird behavior, but in fact permissions now apply only to files installed by Apple's installers. See the following Apple support article: support.apple.com/kb/HT1452.

If an Application Crashes

When an application crashes, it usually occurs in one of two ways: the program disappears abruptly, or it becomes unresponsive. In the first case, you should see a dialog that gives you the option of sending a crash report to Apple (which is a good idea; no personal identifying data is sent along). Restart the application. If it crashes again, consider restarting the computer or using the general troubleshooting advice from earlier.

 Mac OS X uses protected memory, which means that when one application crashes, it doesn't bring down the rest of the machine.

Force quit

If the program is not responding, you'll probably also see the infamous SPOD—Spinning Pizza of Death, the rainbow-colored wheel that replaces the mouse pointer to indicate that Mac OS X is busy processing something. In this case, try force-quitting the program using one of the following methods:

▪ Control-click the application's icon in the Dock and choose Force Quit (**Figure 12.2**). If the menu item reads just "Quit," hold the Option key to invoke the Force Quit option.

Figure 12.2
Force Quit from the Dock.

- If the Dock icon isn't working, go to the Apple menu and choose Force Quit, or press Command-Option-Esc. A dialog appears that shows running applications. Select one and click the Force Quit button.

- Open the Activity Monitor application (located in the Utilities folder), which reports on all of the running processes, including software running invisibly in the background. Select the dead program (listed in red) and click the Quit Process button.

note If the Finder appears to be the problem, you can't force-quit it; the Finder must always be running. Instead, Force Quit is replaced by Relaunch in the Dock and the Force Quit dialog. Choosing Relaunch quits the Finder and brings it back up again.

Delete preferences

If a program is crashing repeatedly, try deleting its preferences file(s). In your Home folder, open the Library folder and then open the Preferences folder. Most application preferences are stored in files here.

1. Quit the application if it's running.

2. Locate the one belonging to your troublesome program—for example, the preferences file for iCal is called "com.apple.iCal.plist," and there's another related file called "com.apple.iCal.helper.plist" (**Figure 12.3**).

Figure 12.3
Locating preference files.

3. Send the file to Trash (drag it to the Trash or press Command-Delete).

4. Relaunch the application. It will automatically create a new prefer-ences file set to the program's defaults.

If You Can't Connect to the Internet

Web sites sometimes go offline and Internet service providers experience snags, but the difficulty could also be in your computer. Try these steps for regaining network access.

1. Open a new Safari window and attempt to access a Web page. If there's no connection, you'll see a warning.

2. Click the Network Diagnostics button on that page to launch a utility of the same name (**Figure 12.4**).

Figure 12.4
Locating preference files.

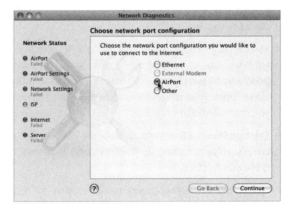

3. Choose an interface for connecting to the Internet and click Continue.

4. Follow the rest of the instructions provided by Network Diagnostics (which vary depending on the nature of the problem).

tip Is your Mac regularly connecting to the wrong network interface? For example, your MacBook Pro is plugged into Ethernet at your office, but it's actually getting network access via AirPort. You can choose which services have priority over others. In the Network preference pane, click the Action menu below the list of interfaces and choose Set Service Order. In the dialog that appears, drag the services to change their order, with the highest priority interface at the top; click OK to exit. Mac OS X will then use your preferred network type first.

Startup Modes

Starting up your computer offers several troubleshooting opportunities, depending on how you do it.

■ **Choose a startup disk.** If you have multiple disks that can run the computer (including a Boot Camp partition running Windows), hold Option at startup to display icons for each disk. Double-click one to start up from it.

■ **Start up in FireWire Target Disk mode.** With two Macs connected via FireWire, you can run one as if it were just an external drive. This is a good way to run Disk Utility on a startup disk without locating the Snow Leopard install disc. Press and hold the T key during startup until you see a large FireWire icon.

■ **Start up from a CD or DVD.** To force the Mac to use an inserted CD or DVD (such as the Snow Leopard installer) as the startup disk, hold the C key during startup.

■ **Eject a disk at startup.** Do you have a recalcitrant disc that won't come out of your Mac's media drive? Unless it's physically jammed in there, restart your computer and hold the mouse button (or trackpad button) during startup to force the drive's eject mechanism.

- **Start up with login items disabled.** This technique is good for trouble-shooting whether a background process is interfering with some other software. Hold Shift as you start up to boot into a stripped-down safe mode.

- **Start up in single-user mode.** If you're having problems even getting to the login stage, hold Command-S during startup to boot into single-user mode. This is a bare-bones, text-only mode that accepts Unix commands. At the command prompt, type:

  /sbin/fsck -fy

  That command performs a disk check as if you were running Disk Utility. Single-user mode is really designed for programmers or for troubleshooting problems that may be interfering with Snow Leopard's startup process.

> **tip** The latest 13-inch and 15-inch MacBook Pro models, introduced in June 2009, feature a built-in SD memory card reader for easily importing photos from a digital camera or camcorder. But it has another capability: if you insert a card and format it with a GUID partition table, you can then install Mac OS X on it and use the SD card as a bootable volume. That means you can carry an emergency boot disk in your wallet or purse!

Support Resources

Remember, there's a lot of help out there for you if you need it.

- **Apple Support:** www.apple.com/support/

- **Apple Support Discussions:** discussions.apple.com

- **Apple Retail Stores:** www.apple.com/retail/

  Schedule a free appointment with an Apple Genius, or get personalized training with the One to One program (when you buy a new Mac).

- **Apple phone support:**

  USA: 1-800-APL-CARE (1-800-275-2273)

  Canada: 1-800-263-3394

  Worldwide: www.apple.com/support/contact/phone_contacts.html

- **Apple Consultant Network:** consultants.apple.com

Should You Purchase AppleCare?

I get this question whenever Apple releases new computers. When you buy a new Mac, you get one year of AppleCare, Apple's warranty service. It doesn't cover accidents like dropping a MacBook Pro onto the floor, but it does address things like a faulty logic board (as my mother-in-law recently discovered). You can extend that warranty to three years from the date you purchased the computer by buying AppleCare as an extended warranty.

I normally hate extended warranties—they always seem like they're designed to rip you off. And yet, nearly all of my Macs have benefitted from having AppleCare beyond the one-year warranty period. So my general advice is to purchase AppleCare for laptops but not desktops, since laptops tend to have smaller, more sensitive electronics and are transported more often.

If you are going to buy AppleCare, you must do it before the first year warranty expires.

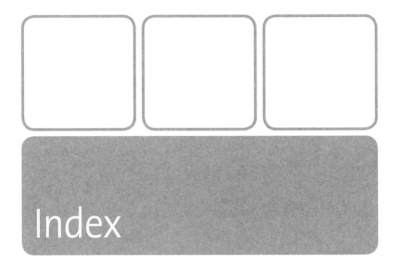

Index